MIKE HAYDEN of San Mateo is a twenty-year veteran of outdoor, travel, and conservation writing and photography. He is
qualified for the job.

Mike Hayden stories and articles and photographs have ap-
peared in recent years in *Field and Stream, Sports Afield, Popular
Mechanics, Outdoor Life, Western Outdoors, The Fisherman,
Outdoors, Better Camping Guide, Saltwater Sportsman, National
Motorist, Westways, Ford Times, Sports Review, Travel,* and
Sportfishing. Mike Hayden photo credits have appeared in *Sunset,
True, American Forest,* innumerable house organs, trade journals,
brochures, and hardcover cooks including *Beautiful California.*
He is also author of the popular Ward Ritchie Press books *Guide-
book To the Northern California Coast, Volume I and Volume II,*
and *Guidebook To the Lake Tahoe Country, Volume I and Volume II.*

Snodgrass Slough off Deadhorse Island.

GUIDEBOOK TO THE SACRAMENTO DELTA COUNTRY

Houseboating, fishing, trails, folklore and legends

BY MIKE HAYDEN

WARD RITCHIE PRESS · LOS ANGELES

This book is dedicated to
Ira E. Charmak.

The material in this book is reviewed and updated
at each printing.

CONTENTS

*Now a quiet, respectable place, Locke in the 1920's
was filled with bars, bordellos, and gambling
dens. This is Levee Street.*

I INTRODUCTION

"The Delta and the bay together constitute a single ecological system. The transition from the fresh waters of the rivers to the salt waters of the bay has produced one of the continent's richest estuarine environments. Salmon, striped bass and steelhead swim up from the ocean and the bay into the Delta and its tributaries. Migratory birds and hundreds of forms of marine and estuarine life swarm in the tidal marshes where each species finds the precisely proper proportions of fresh and salt water."

SUNDAY EXAMINER & CHRONICLE by Harold Gilliam, 1969

One hour by car from San Francisco or a few minutes drive from Sacramento, Stockton, or Tracy, you discover the Delta Country—a thousand square miles of diked islands, elevated levee roads, and twisting, interlocking waterways where the Sacramento and San Joaquin Rivers meet on the floor of the Central Valley.

The Delta Country is not signed or shown in any detail on most road maps. To define its limits on a small scale map, you may pencil in straight lines to link up Antioch, Tracy, Stockton, and Sacramento. This guidebook will cover the area bound by these cities and also neighboring Suisun Bay where the rivers join to form a broad estuary.

It takes time to know the Delta. No freeways cross it. Most of its rural roads and navigable waterways are such as to invite a leisurely pace of exploration. Then too, being flat farm country with few visible landmarks, the Delta is slow to reveal its charms. As one Delta visitor was heard to remark, the enchantment is "a lot of little things." The delight is to discover them one by one.

On the waterways, things like patches of morning mist drifting across the mirror surface of a sunken island where fishermen huddle in flat-bottomed skiffs waiting for a striped bass to bite. A turtle basking on a log in a quiet backwater covered with water hyacinths. The whistle of a tugboat signaling for a drawbridge to open. An outboard towing a water skier up a winding slough fringed with tule reeds. People waving from a houseboat stranded on a sandbar by the ebb tide. A sailing yacht anchored off a wooded islet.

Along the levees, things like quail skittering across the road for the cover of a blackberry thicket. Children spilling out from a school bus to crowd a small country store signed with Chinese characters. The fragrance of magnolia wafted from the grounds of a stately Victorian river mansion. The feeble flicker of an old neon beer sign on an unpainted shanty cafe leaning over a canal on pilings. Tame geese chasing a collie dog off a ferry landing. A grinning man in a yellow slicker waiting to have his picture taken next to a dockside scaffold hung with a five-foot sturgeon.

On the islands, things like a redwing blackbird swooping low over a marshy pond or a muskrat swimming across a drainage ditch. The distant whine of a farm tractor stirring up a storm of peat dust. Field hands on a misty dawn spreading out on the rows to weed sugar beets. Women sorting tomatoes aboard a huge mechanical harvester. A boy walking along the railroad tracks with a string of catfish. A young couple parked off the road in an open sports car, entranced by the optical illusion of a tall ocean steamer plowing through a cornfield.

Such apparitions may startle the traveler, but the Delta's most potent magic is its power to generate nostalgia. More than anything, the lure of the Delta seems to come from what one observer described as a "looks-like-everywhere-else geography." When

Samuel Goldwyn, Jr., was asked why he chose to film "Huckleberry Finn" on some Delta waterways, he replied it was because they "look more like the Mississippi than the real thing."

Millions of people who haven't visited California's Delta Country have seen pieces of it in motion pictures, such as "All the Kings Men," "Porgy and Bess," "Blood Alley," and "Cool Hand Luke." Since the filming of "Steamboat Round the Bend" in the early 1930's, the Delta has provided a location for dozens of motion pictures and television serials with a Midwest, Deep South, or foreign setting.

Oddly though, the Delta, as the Delta, has yet to inspire a movie or major work of fiction. Well-meaning publicists have tried to promote the Delta as "America's Holland," "California's Bayou," and "Everglades of the West." None of these names have stuck. Perhaps because a region filled with bits and pieces of "everywhere else" has to be positively unique—a world apart. You'll find the Delta lingering in the backwash of a history as colorful and exciting as any part of California.

It's part of a legend that two of Cortez' soldiers saw the Delta in 1520. This might have happened and gone unremarked because the Delta Country was then a dismal, mosquito-infested swamp blanketed with tule reeds. The only dry land consisted of natural levees and brushy islets forested with oaks, cottonwood, and yellow pines. Half the Indian population of the Central Valley lived here for it teemed with fish and all kinds of game, including deer, antelope, elk, and vast numbers of ducks and geese.

Historians believe the first Europeans to see the Delta were a small party led by Pedro Fages and Fray Juan Crespi who tried to approach Point Reyes by hiking overland from the east shore of San Francisco Bay. On March 30, 1772, the men reached a promontory on Mount Diablo from which they gazed down on a sheet of water three times the size of Lake Tahoe. This was the

Delta Country flooded by the tide and a heavy spring run-off from the Sierra.

The Spanish explored portions of the Delta by land and water and then wrote it off as a treacherous everglade, unbearably hot in summer. Occasional forays were made to capture Indians for labor. That was all until 1828, when the mountain man, Jedediah Smith, trapped otter, mink, and beaver on the fringes of the Delta. The same year, Smith blazed a trail north to link California with Oregon. At Fort Vancouver, he sold his pelts to the factor of the Hudson Bay Company who was all ears for Smith's account of the Delta.

Thereafter, from 1830 until 1845, the Delta Country was virtually a British protectorate. Fur parties led by Michel LaFramboise, of the Hudson Bay Company, made annual treks down Smith's trail to French Camp near the present site of Stockton. Perhaps just for the fun of it, the trappers joined the Indians on raids against the coastal settlements. They also clashed with trappers working out of Sutter's Fort where Sacramento was founded.

In the 1840's, farmers known as "rim landers" settled on the periphery of the Delta to raise wheat and run cattle. Soon, sailing ships were navigating the Delta to deliver supplies and take on cargoes of hides and tallow. Then came the Gold Rush and, with it, the proud paddlewheel steamers which were to operate in the Central Valley for almost a century.

Their decks bulging with Forty Niners, the sleek sidewheelers sailed to Stockton, Sacramento, and points far beyond the Delta. Shallow-draft steamers made regular runs as far north as Red Bluff on the Sacramento River and as far south as Sycamore Point near Fresno on the San Joaquin River. From Sycamore Point, the distance by steamer to Red Bluff was six hundred miles.

In 1850, miners from the diggings began drifting into the

10

Delta to settle on houseboats or whatever dry land they could find. Shortly, the work of reclaiming the marsh for agriculture began—a task that wasn't completed until the 1930's. Before dredges and other machinery became available, thousands of Chinese were employed to build the levees with shovel and wheelbarrow. Every few years, a winter flood would break through dikes and the Delta would revert to swamp. But, in good years, the immensely fertile peat soil of the islands would deliver fantastic yields of grain, fruits, and vegetables.

The society which evolved on the Delta islands was nearly as feudal as the ante-bellum South. The farms were huge, owing to the large amounts of capital required to reclaim the land. Wealthy farmers in the Sacramento Delta lived, plantation style, in towering mansions. Many farms in the San Joaquin Delta were the property of absentee landowners. The Chinese who furnished most of the labor were treated no better than serfs. The same was true for the various ethnic groups who succeeded them—Japanese, Hindus, Filipinos, and Mexican nationals.

Today, the farms are still huge and growing bigger, but the traveler finds the Delta in the throes of an industrial revolution. The harvesting of crops that, just a few years ago, required the labor of thousands of migratory workers is now performed by a handful of skilled people operating sophisticated machines.

To navigate the Delta by automobile, you drive miles of winding levee roads and leap frog from island to island on ferries and drawbridges. The Delta contains many small islands—sandy reaches, slivers of marsh known as tule berms, and some wooded islets covering no more than a few acres. But most dry land is found on thirty diked islands which range in size from 800 acres to one hundred square miles. These are farmed to produce asparagus, tomatoes, sugar beets, and at least thirty other crops worth $175 million in a good year.

The islands are criss-crossed with drainage ditches and surrounded by an intricate network of canals, cuts, sloughs, and river channels. Stretched end to end, it's estimated these waterways would reach from San Francisco to New York. About seven hundred miles of channels are navigable for pleasure cruisers and houseboats. Ocean freighters thread the islands on two deep water channels to approach the inland ports of Stockton and Sacramento.

Aside from a few small hummocks, the only ground you find in the Delta that rises perceptibly above sea level is on the levees. Behind these great dikes of peat, sand, and river silt, the reclaimed land of the islands lies six to twenty feet below the waterways. For irrigation, the farmer has only to activate a siphon or raise a sluice gate and the river comes pouring in.

You needn't drive far on the islands to discover the levees are the focus of all activity in the Delta. State Highway 160 and most county roads run on them. The scattered farm houses, trailer parks, and sleepy river towns nestle directly behind the levees, which is about the only place on the islands available for settlement. Elsewhere, the light, spongy peat soil will not bear the weight of many buildings. Anchored on the river side of the levees are the floating docks of more than one hundred resorts and marinas where the Delta's fleet of 60,000 pleasure boats are berthed.

In a boat, you may go almost anywhere in the Delta, including some beautiful areas not accessible by road. At least eighty landings have fishing skiffs and outboard motors for rent and quite a few rent mobile houseboats equipped with all the amenities of a well-appointed house trailer. There are scores of places where a towed boat may be launched. But, for a first look at the Delta, the levee roads which run upwards to thirty feet above the waterways and fifty feet above the islands afford the best vantage points to see the country.

In the chapters which follow, this guidebook will chart a three hundred mile drive on which you may sample every corner of the Delta—in a day or two—or much longer if you enjoy camping, fishing, boating, watersports, or exploring obscure rural byways.

The book will include some angling lore because there isn't a body of fresh water in the West which can surpass the Delta for the sheer variety of fish it contains. The game species will be listed, together with some brief exposition on tackle and fishing methods. A few possibilities for duck and pheasant shooting will be mentioned.

The book will cover the resorts, citing those with boat rentals, campgrounds, and parks for trailers and recreational vehicles. Touring the Delta with a trailer presents problems—unless you leave it at a resort—because some levee roads are quite narrow and a special permit may be required to use the ferries. Almost all the resorts have a hoist or ramp for boat launching.

Most Delta resorts are fairly rustic. Those with overnight accommodations—housekeeping cabins, mobile homes, and such—are primarily intended for guests who plan to stay for a few days. Good places to soak up the Delta atmosphere are the small old-fashioned hotels at Rio Vista and Isleton where fruit buyers, shippers, cannery representatives, and others who do business with farmers usually stay. Conventional motels are found in the towns which lie on the periphery of the Delta, including Rio Vista, Lodi, and Tracy.

As for the best time to tour the Delta, it has to be a toss-up between April and May, when the fishing peaks, and the peak harvest months of September and October. Both times, the Delta usually enjoys many warm, sunny days. The river channels serve to moderate the extremes of temperature found elsewhere in the Valley. Even so, summer days are apt to get uncomfortably hot, although the evenings are usually cool. As the Valley warms up in spring, strong winds come blasting in from the Golden Gate to churn up peat dust in the fields and whitecaps on the main waterways.

The Delta has ten frost-free months and receives 14 to 20 inches of rain, most of which falls in winter. January is for fanatics who water ski in rubber suits or brave the tule fogs for an opportunity to hook a granddaddy striped bass.

Ringed by cities with five million people, the miracle of the Delta is that it remains a world apart. Freeways, industry, and tract homes intrude on its borders, but the water-logged peat soil — eighty feet deep in places — frustrates urbanization of the islands. Still, the Delta faces an uncertain future. Perhaps the fate of fabled Atlantis, for ever so slowly the islands are sinking, the dikes are aging, and the top soil is being lost to the winds.

Flat, low-keyed, and deceptively simple, the Delta takes time to know but you need only spend a few hours on the levee roads to enjoy it. In the chapter which follows, we begin our tour where an arm of San Francisco Bay squeezes through a gorge in the Coast Range to meet the Delta at the foot of brooding Mount Diablo.

2 SUISUN BAY

"Benicia is a comic-opera town that ranks with the all-time losers, a Fibber McGee's closet of a town, bursting with yesterday's artifacts, crammed with undiscovered nostalgia. Once named Francisca when men of vision knew that a town that carried the name of the bay would develop into an international port, she lost out to San Francisco." SUNDAY EXAMINER & CHRONICLE by Margot Patterson Doss, 1972

From San Francisco, it takes about twenty minutes (if you miss the commuter rush) to approach the cantilever bridge where Interstate Highway 80 spans the Carquinez Strait. Here is the river-worn gap in the Coast Range — six miles long and about 4,600 feet wide at its narrowest point — through which Pacific tides push salt water into the Central Valley as far east as Antioch.

Our tour begins very near the Carquinez Bridge where we leave the freeway at an exit signed "Crockett." The drive from this exit to Antioch — "The Gateway to the Delta" — is 25 miles.

On the first part of the drive, we'll follow the Carquinez Strait to its confluence with Suisun Bay off Martinez. Then, after a look at the bay, we'll swing inland a few miles and proceed east to Antioch on State Highway 4.

By reason of its location and geography, Suisun Bay is more akin to the Delta Country than to the San Francisco Bay Area. It's isolated from the main population centers of the Bay Area by the highlands of the Diablo Range. Then too, it adjoins primitive marshland which a Hollywood director might find "looks more like the Delta than the real thing!"

From the freeway exit, we turn right on Pomona Street and

shortly pass through the dilapidated village of Crockett. Once a bustling, diversified port, Crockett's sole industry today is the C & H Sugar Refinery. Part of the plant is housed in an antique factory built on the waterfront as a flour mill during the 1880's. Steamers dock at the plant to unload cane from Hawaii.

East of town, Pomona Street climbs and dips on a steep brushy slope overlooking the Carquinez Strait. It's about two miles to the side road which drops down to Port Costa.

From the 1880's until the early 1930's, Port Costa was one of the world's largest grain ports. Now, it's a hamlet filled with craft and antique shops, two stylish restaurants, and a well-preserved hotel, built shortly after Port Costa was founded as a station on the Southern Pacific Railroad in 1879.

Proceeding east on Pomona Street, we pass White's Resort, a rustic landing with boats and motors for rent. In winter, people gather on the wharf here to fish for starry flounder.

Towering ahead is the Benicia-Martinez Toll Bridge which replaced the Benicia Ferry when it was completed in 1962. The bridge crosses Carquinez Strait where it opens to Suisun Bay.

Suisun Bay, ranging to six miles in width, is a complicated spread of water because it combines the features of a bay, a lake, a river, and tidal marsh. The elongated portion of the bay — the part which stretches from Carquinez Strait 22 miles to the mouth of the Delta near Antioch — represents the combined flow of the Sacramento and San Joaquin Rivers. This great waterway is filled with shoals and low marshy islands. It was a graveyard for many sailing ships at the time of the Gold Rush. Since then, ship channels 300 feet wide have been dredged.

The shallowest water — ranging from a few feet to only inches deep — is found on the north side of the bay in Honker and Grizzly Bays. These bays adjoin the Suisun Marshes. Here is a semi-wilderness of twisting sloughs and swampy islands which recall the Delta Country before it was reclaimed for agriculture.

People come here to fish for catfish and striped bass and to hunt ducks and pheasant on state land that's planted with barley. The boat landings, launching ramps, and shooting grounds are approached on the Grizzly Island Road which leaves State Highway 12 near Fairfield.

The water in Suisun Bay is brackish, with a much lower salt content than the ocean. Historians speculate "Suisun" was the name of an Indian village situated on or near the bayshore.

Three miles east of White's Resort, the Pomona Road terminates at a junction with Alhambra Avenue in Martinez.

Founded in 1849, Martinez is the seat of Contra Costa County. It was named for a commandante of the San Francisco Presidio who obtained this townsite at the mouth of the Alhambra Valley as part of a land grant known as Rancho El Pinole. No longer a quiet farm center and fishing port, the town reflects the mushroom growth of residential communities in the hills behind it. John Muir's old home still stands at Alhambra Avenue and Franklin Canyon Road.

On the waterfront are marinas, a boat ramp, and the refinery wharves of the Shell Oil Company. East from Martinez to Pittsburg, the bayshore is too marshy to support a shoreline drive. The so-called Waterfront Road leaves the foot of Alhambra Avenue to approach Port Chicago, site of a naval ammunition depot. Port Chicago used to be a town until a few years ago when the navy evicted its 1,900 residents.

Three miles from Martinez across the toll bridge is Benicia, founded in 1846 by General Mariano Vallejo. This town is filled with relics, including some homes which date back to 1849. The outstanding attraction—now a state historic monument—is a brick building fronted by Doric columns which, for a year, served as the state capitol. Governor John Bigler moved the capitol to Sacramento in 1854.

Benicia grew to prominence as a way station on the road to

17

the Mother Lode. It was also a coaling station for paddlewheel steamers and, for more than a century, the site of a huge military arsenal. The old arsenal is presently being developed as a waterfront industrial park.

West of Benicia off Interstate Highway 680 is the Benicia State Recreation Area, a picnic spot on the Carquinez Strait popular with fishermen who plug cast for striped bass.

From Martinez, we motor east on State Highway 4. After ten miles, the first of many smoking industrial plants becomes visible in the direction of the bayshore. P. G. & E., Kaiser, Dow, U. S. Steel, Continental Can are a few of the companies which dominate the skyline of Pittsburg and neighboring Antioch.

In 1849, when he was 29 years old, William Tecumseh Sherman laid out the "City of New York of the Pacific." The port was renamed "Black Diamond" in the 1850's after it became a shipping point for coal mined on the slopes of Mount Diablo. Competition forced the mines to close in the 1880's, but the port survived as a fishing village until it acquired a steel mill around 1910. A little later, the name of the town was changed to Pittsburg.

Antioch was founded in 1849 as Smith's Landing by two brothers, both ministers, who organized a party of settlers to come here by ship from New England. Two years later, the name was changed to Antioch at a picnic attended by the town's forty residents. For a time, Antioch was the port for the Empire Coal Mine. Later, it acquired importance as a shipping point for farm produce. Eastern Contra Costa is still a major growing area for almonds, walnuts, cut-flowers, and other specialty crops.

About fourteen miles east of Martinez, we leave Highway 4 to approach Antioch's business district, which is quiet and pleasantly obsolete. At the foot of H Street is a public fishing pier. This adjoins the Riverview Lodge, a popular seafood restaurant

*Suisun Bay in January. One of the loveliest
state parks in Northern California lies at the
summit of Mount Diablo.*

which has picture windows looking out on the Stockton Ship Channel.

Antioch is a favorite port of embarkation for Delta waterways. A profusion of dockside facilities — boat ramps, bait shops, marinas — are found off Wilbur Avenue in the vicinity of the Antioch Bridge. Two liveries which rent houseboats are the S & H Boatyard and Lauritzen Yacht Harbor. The Fulton Shipyard Road off Wilbur Avenue approaches a marina and public launching ramp.

Martinez and Antioch each have a motel and Pittsburg has two. The public boat ramp at Pittsburg and several marinas located west of the city are convenient to some good fishing on upper Suisun Bay. Catfish and striped bass are most frequently hooked, but some fantastic mixed catches have been reported. In a few hours time, one man fishing with sardine bait off Pittsburg caught a flounder, a catfish, a steelhead trout, a king salmon, a sturgeon, and three striped bass.

Striper fishing on Suisun Bay is usually best from late July through December. Often though, during this period, small craft warnings may be hoisted at Antioch's warning display station. In the early days, sailing vessels were sometimes forced by the winds to hole up at Antioch or New York of the Pacific for as long as a week.

Across the ship channel from Antioch is Sherman Island. Just off the marshy tip of this large island, the narrow neck of Suisun Bay forms a Y junction with the main channels of the Sacramento and San Joaquin Rivers. This is considered the mouth of the Delta.

3 SHERMAN ISLAND

*"Sherman Island has 15,000 acres enclosed within the levees.
Generally potatoes are first planted, and after that with beans,
so that two crops are raised per year. A great many either rent
their farms on shares or for a round sum per acre. One man
receives $15 an acre and does nothing but collect the rent."*

ILLUSTRATIONS OF CONTRA COSTA COUNTY
by Smith & Ellito, 1879

When the Antioch Bridge was built in 1925, it was acclaimed an
engineering marvel—the largest highway bridge in the West.
It's still a delight for the traveler because it affords a spectacu-
lar view of the Delta. But the local feeling about this drawbridge which links Antioch with Sherman Island is such that, in
1972, the legislature voted to replace it with a larger span.

The bridge is important to the Delta economy because it's
the only place outside Stockton where the ship channel of the
San Joaquin River may be crossed by automobile. State Highway 160 leaves Antioch on the bridge to follow the main channel of the Sacramento River 55 miles to the state capitol.

A tall slender structure, nearly three-quarters of a mile long,
the bridge supports a narrow roadway which crests 70 feet above
the ship channel. The vertical lift span may be raised to provide
a clearance of 135 feet at high tide.

The bridge was closed to traffic for eleven months after
Sherman Island was flooded in 1969—and for five months in
1970-71 after it was struck by a freighter navigating in a tule fog.
The collision jammed the lift span in the raised position, trapping
the lift operator in the control cabin for eighteen hours. Since
then, several bridge tenders have turned down offers of a job on
the span. But the lonely shifts in the control room seem not to

21

bother Mrs. Ruby Vanderhave, who may be the only female lift span operator in the United States.

The reclaimed portion of Sherman Island measures 7½ miles long and up to three miles wide. The island was named for Sherman Day, the U. S. Surveyor General for California in 1868-71. Probably the first person to farm the island was Robert E. Beasley, a "rim lander" who settled on the west bank of the Sacramento River near Tolan's Landing in 1851.

Beasley established a ferry which ran from his place to Sherman Island when it was still in the public domain. Neither the Spanish nor Mexican governors made land grants covering any of the islands. There was no private ownership until the state legislature authorized the sale of Delta marsh for $1.00 an acre. This happened in 1855 after California assumed control of the Delta from the federal government under provisions of the 1850 Swamp and Overflow Act.

At first, the most swampland an individual could buy was 320 acres. In 1859, the quota was raised to 640 acres. Then, shortly after the state gave control of the Delta to the counties in 1866, all restrictions were lifted and the speculators moved in. One man bought 153 square miles of swamp. By 1871, almost all of the Delta was spoken for.

An act in 1861 provided for the state to organize reclamation districts and assign engineers to drain the islands. But, as of 1885, only 8,000 acres in the Delta were effectively reclaimed and flood-free. About 1870, a crew of Chinese were employed to improve the dikes on Sherman Island. After the work was completed in 1872, some Chinese remained to work the land as tenant farmers. But, when the dikes broke in the flood of 1878, the Chinese moved to Staten Island.

From the Antioch Bridge, the highway cuts across the interior of Sherman Island where we see no trees or dwellings—just acres of crops and freshly plowed peat soil. About a mile farther,

22

we come to a parking area at the foot of the levee which encloses Mayberry Slough. This is good water to bank fish for catfish and largemouth black bass.

Four miles farther, the highway climbs to the levee which fronts Horseshoe Bend on the Sacramento River. We turn left here on the West Levee Road and shortly pass a farmhouse on stilts and the mouldering docks of an old boat livery. Across Horseshoe Bend, we see part of the Rio Vista Army Depot's mothball fleet anchored off Decker Island.

The levee bends south to meet the main channel of the Sacramento where it's half a mile wide. The rolling grasslands across the river are known as the Montezuma Hills. Geologists believe they were built up from deposits of river silt and later deformed by folding and faulting.

The water directly off the West Levee Road is one of the favorite places to fish in the Delta. On any balmy day in spring, the river here will be dotted with skiffs working bait for striped bass. There are numerous sidings on the road where bank fishermen park and climb down the levee to cast off the berms. Some stripers are hooked from shore, but mostly catfish are caught.

Four kinds of catfish are found in the Delta, of which the white catfish (*ictalurus catus*) accounts for 95% of the catch. Averaging nine inches in length, catfish may be taken in the Delta with any tackle stout enough to handle one- to three-ounce bank sinkers. Such weights are needed because of the strong currents in most waterways. The preferred terminal rig is a three-foot leader, with two dropper loops for snelled No. 2 or No. 4 hooks and a swivel snap for the sinker. Sardines and fresh water clams are popular baits.

Before commercial fishing ended in 1953, some Delta residents made as much as $1,000 a week catching catfish with fyke nets. These were the last of the true "river rats" who lived near their nets in houseboats or waterfront shanties.

23

Delta farmers rotate their crops but never let the rich peat soil lie fallow for long. After this field of corn on Sherman Island is harvested, it will probably be sown with barley, milo, or alfalfa.

24

About three miles down the road, we descend from the levee on an unpaved spur which winds past a sandy beach through alder thickets to the Blind Point Fishing Access. The public boat ramp here is convenient to Sherman Lake—a 3,100-acre tract that was flooded years ago and never reclaimed. Now a state wildlife refuge, it's one of the better places to fish for stripers in winter. Duck hunting is legal on Sherman Lake in season.

Returning to Highway 160, it's a mile up the levee to the Beanpot Resort, which has rowboats on two ponds filled with bass and sunfish. Two miles farther, we arrive at the vertical lift bridge which crosses Three Mile Slough to Brannan Island. We turn right here on the East Levee Road and follow the slough a mile to the Outrigger. This attractive marina, perched on a tree-shaded point opposite Twitchell Island, caters mainly to yachtsmen. Two miles farther, the road turns south where it meets the broad channel of the San Joaquin.

Visible behind the levee on this drive are several barns and farmhouses, remarkable only for the extraordinary amount of machinery clustered about them. There are machines for tilling, seeding, planting, spraying, dusting, baling, and harvesting. The huge investment this equipment represents is one reason many Delta farms—including family-owned farms and the so-called "independents"—are organized as corporations.

Shortly, we arrive at Eddo's Boat Harbor, which might serve as a prototype for scores of Delta resorts. Typically, the floating docks anchored below the levee enjoy the protection of a natural breakwater—a long, low marshy berm covered with brush and tule reeds. The quiet waterway that runs between the berm and the levee is known as Gallagher Slough.

Eddo's rents rowboats for $5 and skiffs with motors for $14. Some skiffs have little cabins for windy days; these cost a dollar extra. Houseboats will be covered in another chapter, but Eddo's

THREE MUSKETEERS
FISING RESORT BAIT
BOATS MOTORS CAFE
PIER FISHING 50¢ POLE
CAMPING   OPIN

Sherman Island.

has several for rent by the day or the week. For much of the year, resorts, such as Eddo's, depend heavily on the custom of week-enders from the Bay Area. But a growing source of income is the rental of moorage to boat owners. Eddo's has ten covered berths and fifty open berths. There is an ice box, fish rack, and gas pump on the dock.

Other dockside facilities include a bait shop, snack bar, and boat ramp. Fishing tackle may be rented and the services of a guide may be arranged for. Behind the levee, Eddo's has space for a hundred boat trailers, and grounds for picnics, tent camping, and recreational vehicles. There is a shower room and small store. Some Delta resorts have invested heavily in luxury mobile homes, which may be rented for periods as short as a weekend. Quite a number of resorts have restaurants and a few have bars.

Many people living in the San Francisco Bay Area can remember when to rent a boat in the Delta was to persuade a farmer, for a few dollars, to loan his rowing skiff. The resorts today mostly began within the last twenty or thirty years as small "Mom and Pop" landings where the customer was often required to furnish his own outboard motor. Some places have grown faster than others—but good, poor, modest, or expensive, the style of nearly all Delta resorts is rustic and family-oriented.

Bearing south on the East Levee Road, the berm which protects Eddo's Harbor soon ends and the San Joaquin River returns to view where it's almost a mile wide. There are good places along the levee to bank fish or sit and watch the river traffic. But the pavement is narrow and parking space is hard to find. After a mile or so, the road leaves the levee to rejoin Highway 160.

Spacious campground at Brannon Island State Park has sites for tents, trailers, and camper wagons.

4 RIO VISTA

"The other day was overcast with a threat of rain in the dull sky. The River was quiet and smooth. The pear orchards under the levees had that late-fall, cold, limp look. The drowned tomato fields were dank. Blackbirds swirled in great flocks over the canals and overhead wide V's of geese swept along, heading south. Hunters were walking some of the stubble fields. They looked cold and walked slowly."

THE SAN FRANCISCO CHRONICLE by Henry Schacht, 1964

Three Mile Slough, which divides Brannan Island from Sherman Island, is one of the most traveled waterways in the Delta. This is because it provides a convenient interchange for the main channels of the Sacramento and San Joaquin Rivers. Barges and tugboats sometimes use it as a shortcut. Also contributing to the traffic is the six-lane small boat launching ramp at Brannan Island State Park.

The state park occupies 336 acres of the highest ground in the Delta—a hummock at the southwest corner of Brannan Island. This area, which rises to 25 feet above sea level, was first settled in 1852. The park entrance lies off Highway 160 a short distance from the bridge on Three Mile Slough.

The campground has 100 sites for tents and trailers. Fifteen years ago, the state planted trees and grass here, landscaping the barren rise with such finesse that today it appears to be a natural area. The park has shore fishing, a swimming beach, and sand dunes which invite sun bathing.

North from the park, the river side of the levee is fringed with towering eucalyptus trees. Behind the levee are pear orchards—perhaps not in the best of shape following the 1972 flood which originated from a levee break on neighboring Andrus

Island. Four miles up the road is Harry & Bobbie's, a large resort-type marina with houseboat rentals.

A half-mile farther, the road intersects State Highway 12 at the Rio Vista Bridge. This drawbridge is the busiest on the Sacramento, with 3,000 openings a year for freighters, barges, and large pleasure yachts. The lift span rises 138 feet above water; in the down position, it has a clearance of only thirteen feet.

All bridges on the main channels are manned 24 hours. Those on the smaller sloughs may be manned eight hours or only on special call. Bridges on the more obscure channels of the San Joaquin Delta may require several days' notice to be raised. A vessel approaching a drawbridge signals the tender with three whistle blasts. The tender answers with three blasts of his horn. Then he sets off an alarm to warn motorists and lowers barricades on the approaches to the bridge.

Midway across the Rio Vista Bridge, we pass from Sacramento County to Solano County.

The original site of Rio Vista was a couple miles or so above the bridge where the Sacramento is joined by Cache Slough. Founded in 1857 as Brazos Del Rio (Arms of the River), the town was renamed Rio Vista before it was flooded out in 1862. At its present location on the edge of the Montezuma Hills, Rio Vista has only to worry about its bridge. The span has been hit several times by freighters in recent years.

Rio Vista had the world's largest asparagus cannery before a blight reduced the size of the crop in the western Delta. Since then, the Delta has lost most of its canneries to cities, such as Sacramento, Stockton, and Tracy, which are transportation hubs and afford a better labor supply.

Now a quiet trading center, Rio Vista hungers for industry but displays remarkable signs of affluence for a population of only 3,000. South of the aging business district is "Millionaire

Row," which includes some mansions in the Victorian style. Among the newer structures are the city hall, police station, and municipal swimming pool, all built with royalties derived from one of the largest natural gas fields in the world.

The Rio Vista field first came to public notice in January 1936, when the wildcat "Emigh No. 1" was drilled two miles west of Rio Vista. The field extends well into the Delta. From Brannan Island, a gas line crosses Twitchell and Sherman Islands to the P. G. & E. plant at Antioch. Quite a few Delta farmers have financed a new life style with the income obtained from royalties. Joe Lopes built himself a $75,000 home after he and some friends drilled successfully on his farm at Grand Island. Most leases in the Rio Vista field are held by six large oil companies.

Several dredging companies are based at Rio Vista. The "Marbeet" harvester, manufactured at the Blackwelder Iron Works is said to have saved the sugar beet industry when the bracero program was ended in 1964. South of town is the Rio Vista Army Depot where scores of military support vessels are mothballed. The U. S. Coast Guard has a station at 900 South Second Street.

Next door to City Hall is a public boat ramp convenient to some of the most reliable striped bass water in the Delta—for trolling as well as bait fishing. Late fall through spring is best, but some large stripers are taken every month of the year.

On Main Street is Hap's Bait Store which rents rowboats, fishing skiffs, sailboats, houseboats, and power boats for water skiing. The large, very modern Delta Marina Yacht Harbor on Marina Drive has boat rentals, tent camping, grounds for trailers and recreational vehicles, a new motor lodge, and the Point Restaurant. Another popular place to eat is the Big Horn Restaurant on Main Street. The dining room here contains a bizarre collection of trophy heads, including those of lions, tigers, and an elephant.

From Rio Vista, it's 18 miles by way of Highway 12 and the

31

Collinsville Road to the old port of Collinsville located opposite the confluence of the Sacramento and San Joaquin Rivers. Salmon fishermen of Italian descent used to live here in homes elevated above the tidewater on stilts. The port was named for C. J. Collins, who settled near the site in 1856. In the 1860's, the name was changed to Newport by a promoter who tried to sell lots in a "paper city" covering 2,390 acres of marsh. There were few takers, even when a lot could be had for only $5, and, in 1869, the name was changed back to Collinsville. A salmon cannery was built in 1873.

Collinsville is kept alive by the Collinsville Fishing Resort, a large establishment with rental boats, a store and restaurant, and grounds for trailers, recreational vehicles, and tent camping.

Near Collinsville at the end of Stratton Lane is the Montezuma House, otherwise known as the Hastings Adobe. It was built in 1846 by Landsford W. Hastings, who published "The Emigrant's Guide" and led emigrant parties to California in 1843 and 1845.

From Bird's Landing on the Collinsville Road, a road runs east to connect with the Montezuma Hills Road. This byway affords a slow, winding drive through the sheep country of the hills to Rio Vista.

At Rio Vista Junction eleven miles west of Rio Vista on Highway 12 is a Railway Museum which includes some trains of the old Northern Electric Railroad.

5 RYER ISLAND

"One fact, however, marred the informed passenger's pleasure in the riverboats; their saloons were commonly more satisfactory than their engines, the boilers inferior to the berths. The first twenty years of steam navigation on the Sacramento presented a disconcerting record of founderings, wrecks, and explosions, with a list of victims mounting into the hundreds."

THE BIG FOUR by Oscar Lewis, 1938

From Rio Vista near the waterfront, the Ryer Island Road runs 2½ miles to the ferry landing on Cache Slough.

Maine Prairie Slough was the name for Cache Slough when hay scows and paddlewheel steamers navigated it. At the head of the slough was the busy port of Maine Prairie where Captain J. C. Merithew settled in 1859. The town faded away after the Sacramento Northern Railroad was built.

Cache Slough is one of the largest, longest sloughs in the Delta. Three miles upstream from the ferry is the entrance to the Sacramento Deepwater Ship Channel which runs 22 miles to Lake Washington in West Sacramento. Completed in 1954, the channel is 30 feet deep, 200-300 feet wide, and thirteen miles shorter than the route traveled by tugs and barges up the main channel of the Sacramento.

Sport fishermen hook catfish and stripers in Cache Slough and also quite a few white sturgeon, which are the largest freshwater game fish in North America. In the previous century, teams of horses were used in the Delta to land sturgeon that measured 20 feet and weighed 1,000 pounds. The demand for sturgeon was great because they are an excellent tablefish when broiled, baked, boiled, barbequed, fried, pickled, or smoked. Sturgeon

*Confluence of Cache Slough with Lindsey, Shag,
Prospect, and Miner Sloughs. Islands on Lindsey
Slough are subject to flooding during high water.*

became so rare that the state imposed a closed season in 1917 which was not reopened until 1954.

Now many sturgeon are hooked in the Delta to 40 pounds and some are taken each year to 250 pounds. In April 1972, the Sacramento near Verona yielded a 405-pound sturgeon to Bill McNew of Olivehurst. The battle lasted three hours.

Good tackle for "diamond backs" is a sturdy 6½-foot boat rod and star drag reel spooled with 50-80 pound test monofilament line. A sliding sinker rig is favored with size 4/0-6/0 hooks. One expert recommends a braided steel leader with a 15-inch tippet of heavy monofilament. Sardines, "bullheads," and glass shrimp are popular baits.

Sturgeon, like salmon, steelhead, shad, and striped bass, are anadromous—which is to say, they migrate between the rivers and salt water. Large sturgeon are most common in the Delta from December through May. The legal limit is one fish a day, with a minimum size of 40 inches. The "Weekend Outdoor Map" sold in most Delta bait stores pinpoints many sturgeon holes and good places to fish for other game species.

All public ferries in the Delta are free, but the Ryer Island Ferry is the only "free ferry" in the sense it operates without a cable and requires a licensed navigator at the wheel. A cable isn't feasible on Cache Slough because of the deep draft vessels which pass through it.

Across Cache Slough, we travel on the diesel-powered *Real McCoy* shortly to pull up on the levee of Ryer Island. This large tract was named for Dr. W. M. Ryer, a Stockton physician who vaccinated 2,000 Valley Indians in the summer of 1852. Epidemics of the white man's diseases depopulated the Delta of all but a handful of Indians before the first settlers arrived. By one estimate, the Indian population of the entire Central Valley fell from 83,000 in 1800 to only 19,000 in 1851.

Much acreage on Ryer Island is given to sugar beets, which

are the "bread and butter" crop for many Delta farmers. Observed in the fields, sugar beets resemble market beets except their leaves are green instead of red. Production began in the 1870's but, for years, the Delta crop suffered a low sugar content. Farmers had to cope with various plant diseases and master the science of crop rotation.

Also labor was a problem. For each man employed in the cultivation of wheat, the services of 41½ men were needed for beet culture. Beet sugar refineries sprang up on the perimeter of the Delta after the Dingley Tariff Act of 1897 imposed a heavy duty on imported sugar. But it wasn't until the 1930's Delta farmers achieved a harvest that could match the sugar content of beets grown anywhere else in the world.

In spring, you see labor crews weeding and thinning but, otherwise, beet farming is completely mechanized. The "Marbeet" machine digs the beets, removes the tops, and conveys the beets to trucks moving alongside the harvester. There's little waste. The beet pulp is mixed with molasses to make a cattle feed. The tops may be used for forage or fertilizer.

The levee road, which runs north from the ferry landing, follows Cache and Miner Sloughs to approach the Islands Marina at the mouth of Duck Slough. South on the levee, we round the tip of Ryer Island to the Hidden Harbor Resort on Steamboat Slough. This marina includes boat rentals, camping for recreational vehicles, and a restaurant.

Three miles farther up Steamboat Slough, we come to Snug Harbor Marina which has both tent and vehicle camping.

Paddlewheel steamers on the run between Rio Vista and Sacramento traveled by way of Steamboat Slough because it contained fewer snags and shoals than the main river. Also because it was six miles shorter. Perhaps the first steamer to pass through the slough was the little 40-ton *Sitka* which a San Francisco merchant purchased from the Russians. In 1847, the

Summer home on Steamboat Slough.

Sitka made one round trip to Sacramento before it sank in a storm at its San Francisco pier.

The first large steamers to navigate Steamboat Slough arrived from the East Coast a few months after Marshall discovered gold on the American River. In November 1849, the elegant 750-ton side-wheeler *Senator* began regular service between San Francisco and Sacramento. By 1850, there were 28 steamers operating on the rivers and sloughs. Some of these were propeller ships and broad-beamed stern-wheelers but most were the lean, fast, graceful side-wheelers which predominated on the runs to Stockton and Sacramento through the 1860's.

The side-wheelers were fairly deep-draft vessels (to 9½ feet) with space forward, known as the "China hold," for Oriental passengers. On some boats, the dining room was located aft. On the main deck were offices, staterooms, and cargo space. The second deck was partly given over to the "social hall." On the weather deck was the "Texas" reserved for the ship's officers and V.I.P. passengers. Just forward, or on top of the "Texas," was the pilot house and behind the "Texas" was the walking beam. Some side-wheelers had twin stacks.

Speeding up Steamboat Slough in the winter of 1850-51, the smart side-wheeler *New World* exploded, killing seven persons. The cause was a ruptured steam line, soon repaired, but races between rival boats produced many disasters in the early days. Over fifty people died when the *Pearl* blew up off Marysville in 1855.

Steamboat Slough was a favorite drag strip. One day, the swift *Antelope* tried to pass the *Sacramento* on the slough and was forced inshore by the latter vessel up on a mudbank. Such was the competition that steamship companies hired "runners" to create disturbances on their rival's ships. And there were price wars. For a time, the fare from San Francisco to Sacramento was reduced to ten cents.

38

Steamboat Slough today is strictly a playground for fishermen and water skiers. The largest vessels you see on it are Chinese junks that were built to order for wealthy yachtsmen and the Howard Landing Ferry, a flat-bottomed boat, 62 feet long, which runs to Grand Island.

Private estate on Grand Island.

6 GRAND ISLAND

"The wanton rape of Delta river and slough levees a couple of years ago by the mad axemen of the Army Engineers and local reclamation districts has finally produced—as predicted by opposition sportsmen's groups—a most ugly illegitimate offspring: Erosion."

THE SAN FRANCISCO CHRONICLE by Jack Schmale, 1963

We cross Steamboat Slough to Howard Landing on the ferryboat *J Mack,* which is guided by a cable stretched between Ryer and Grand Islands. While the ferry is at rest, the cable is usually lowered so small boats may cross it safely at slow speeds. But the cable poses a hazard while the ferry is underway. On Memorial Day 1971, three persons in a speedboat died as a result of a collision with the cable.

Maidu Indians were still living on Grand Island when Reuben Kercheval arrived from the diggings, perhaps as early as 1849. Kercheval employed the Indians to build what may have been the first levee in the Delta. Only a few feet high, this dike was constructed with blocks of peat cut from wet ground. When the peat dried, it shrank, leaving crevices which allowed the dike to leak like a sieve in the great flood of 1852.

Kercheval built a larger dike which collapsed in the 1861 flood. It was much the same story in the floods of 1868 and 1872, but Kercheval persisted. He raised a levee eight feet high and 40 feet wide at the base. This dike failed in the 1876 flood. Then Kercheval erected a dike 12 feet high and 100 feet across at the base which was reinforced with sand and river silt. This dike broke in the high water of 1878 and again in 1881. Kercheval didn't live to see Grand Island go under in the 1890 flood. It wasn't until the flood of 1907 the dikes finally held.

41

Kercheval's great enemy, which he fought as a senator in the state legislature, was the mixture of fine silt, sand, and stones, known as "slickens." In 30 years, two billion cubic yards of "slickens" were dumped into the Sacramento River system by hydraulic mining. It was this muck which elevated the river beds faster than the levees could be raised. The problem wasn't abated in the Delta until hydraulic mining was outlawed by the debris act of 1893.

The Maidu people wintered on Grand Island in dome-shaped homes and moved to camps in the uplands when the hot weather set in. They utilized the tules and other reeds of the Delta marsh to make rugs, baskets, mattresses, roofing, duck decoys, and boat-like rafts. They made bread from cat-tails and harvested the tubers of arrow-head, which the Chinese later cultivated under the name of "tule potatoes." Spears, bow and arrow, and bone hooks were employed to take fish.

Apparently, the Maidu of Grand Island perished from an epidemic, possibly smallpox, within a few years of Kercheval's arrival. An old history relates that Dwight Spence, Esq., saw the remains of 500 Indians at Grand Island in 1851. The relationship of the Indians to the Delta settlers seems to have been that of slave to master. Such was the law that an Indian unable to produce a certificate showing he was employed by a white man risked getting shot as a thief.

Scholars may only guess how the Indians divided up the Delta. It was reported the Maidu inhabited Andrus, Tyler, Staten, and Brannan Islands. The Miwok were said to occupy Sherman Island and the area of the Mokelumne River east of Walnut Grove. The Wintuns controlled the Suisun Marshes and the Yokuts lived along the banks of lower San Joaquin clear to the mouth. In 1870, only five Indians remained in San Joaquin County.

Grand Island lies in Sacramento County. From Howard Landing, the road north approaches the "River Mansion," a large restaurant housed in a palatial dwelling. South, about one-half mile down the levee, is Sid's Holiday Harbor. A mile farther is the county-maintained Hogback Island Recreation Area. This attractive tree-shaded berm has a public boat ramp and large picnic area.

Hogback Island was developed in the 1960's by the Army Engineers, who badly needed a show-case project to offset their image as a destroyer of the Delta's beauty.

We've seen trees here and there on the drive thus far. But the levees used to be fringed everywhere with oaks, willows, walnuts, sycamores, and cottonwoods, some of which grew 100 feet tall. These trees not only lent beauty to the waterways, but it was generally believed their roots served to strengthen the levees. The Engineers decided otherwise in the mid-1950's and began knocking down the trees with cranes and bulldozers. They also removed the ground cover of cane, grape, blackberry, and California wild rose.

The Pacific Inter-Club Yacht Association organized a protest against tree stripping which was joined by fishermen, conservationists, and resort owners. At first, the Engineers turned a deaf ear to the outcry but there was also static from county officials who complained tree stripping was causing the roads to wash out.

The Engineers said the trees interfered with the work of renovating the levees and facing them with rock. They also cited the danger of an old tree uprooting in a heavy wind so as to leave a weak spot in the levee. They said ground cover, such as brambles, made it difficult to inspect the levees for weak spots.

Among those who spoke out against tree stripping was the late Erle Stanley Gardner of "Perry Mason" fame who wrote three books about his experiences in the Delta. In one book, Gardner wryly predicted that the Engineers would eventually change their mind about the desirability of trees and "an expensive program of reforestation will be inaugurated."

Sure enough, in 1966, the Engineers began to modify their policies and, in 1972, they announced that trees would be saved wherever possible. Foliage which had to be removed from the levees would be replaced by new trees and shrubs. Experimental seeding and planting would take place at five sites on the Sacramento River downstream from Colusa.

From Hogback Island, we drive around the tip of Grand Island to the main channel of the Sacramento. It's about seven miles to the Isleton Bridge, where we pick up State Highway 160. Nine miles farther is the hamlet of Ryde (population 180) which was named for a town on the Isle of Wright when it was founded in 1892. Ryde was formerly the site of an asparagus cannery built by Libby, McNeil and Libby in 1910.

From Ryde, it's three miles to the city limit of Walnut Grove, which is centered on the east bank of the river. Walnut Grove is quite small yet, oddly, it's the only town south of Red Bluff to occupy both banks of the Sacramento.

Six miles farther, we arrive at the north end of Grand Island where Steamboat Slough joins the main river. On the slough a quarter-mile west of this junction is the Steamboater's Restaurant and Boatel which has houseboats for rent.

7 THE SOUTH RIVER ROAD

"Among the islands and marshes of the delta mink roam wild and are trapped for their pelts. Energetic beavers swim in the delta's marshes and canals, and their excavations are such a menace to the levees that irate farmers have formed a Beaver Control District to curb the damage."

SAN FRANCISCO BAY by Harold Gilliam, 1957

The South River Road affords one of the most pleasant and interesting drives in the Delta. Part of its charm is the views it obtains of the river traffic, which includes tugs and barges as well as pleasure craft.

The barges are of various types designed to transport grain, gravel, oil, caustics, acids, molasses, sugar, produce, and explosives. There are huge container barges which operate on a regular schedule between Sacramento and container terminals on San Francisco Bay. The voyage by barge to the Oakland terminal takes ten hours.

Completed in 1931, the Sacramento Shallow Draft Channel is ten feet deep to Sacramento and six feet deep to Colusa, which is the head of navigation for cruisers and houseboats. The distance by water to Colusa from Antioch is 125 miles.

Some of the first barges on the river were operated by the Sacramento Wood Company in the 1860's. This company contracted for paddlewheel steamers to haul its barges. But the rates charged for this service were so high that, in the 1870's, the company acquired its own steamers and reorganized as the Sacramento Transportation Company. In 1932, the firm joined other companies to form the River Lines, which is still in business.

Paddlewheel navigation beyond the Delta was gradually phased out as the rivers silted in and ever larger amounts of

American Crystal Sugar Refinery at Clarksburg.

water were diverted for industry and agriculture. Passenger and freight service to Marysville on the Feather River ended in 1914. Two years later, regular service to Red Bluff was terminated. The last stern-wheelers called at Colusa in 1932.

From Grand Island, we cross Steamboat Slough to Sutter Island on a drawbridge of the bascule type. This span operates on the same principle as the mechanized gate at a railway crossing, being constructed with a counterweight at the pivot point. On Steamboat Slough near the north end of the bridge is Steamboat Landing which has houseboats for rent.

Sutter Island is three miles long and only half a mile wide. It was first named Schoolcraft Island, probably for H. A. Schoolcraft, an early settler.

It's a mile from Steamboat Slough to the Paintersville Bridge which spans the main river near Courtland. State Route 160 crosses here to the east levee. The South River Road continues up the west levee, shortly to arrive at Sutter Slough. We cross this quiet waterway on a swing bridge to Merritt Island in Yolo County.

From the bridge, a levee road runs up the north bank of Sutter Slough to approach the Tye-A-Lee Docks on Elkhorn Slough. Tye-A-Lee has launching and boat rentals. Black bass abound in Elkhorn Slough which is one of the few places in the Delta where you may still see beaver.

Historians suspect Merritt Island was named for Ezekiel Merritt, a tough backwoodsman who was said to have a hunting camp on the island. Merritt was based for a time at Sutter's Fort and participated in the Bear Flag Revolt.

Before Merritt Island was settled in 1850, it was densely forested with oak trees which were cut down to provide fuel for the paddlewheel steamers.

It's not known precisely when Reuben Kercheval made his first attempt to reclaim Grand Island. But there are documents

47

which show Josiah Green completed a dike on Merritt Island shortly before it was inundated by the 1852 flood. As at Grand Island, the work was accomplished, first with shovel and wheelbarrow, and later with horse and drag shovel. In the 1870's, Josiah Green's sons, Lester and George, rebuilt the levee with the aid of what may have been the first clamshell dredger to operate in the Delta.

From Sutter Slough, it's five miles up the South River Road to the county-maintained Clarksburg Fishing Access. This attractive boat launching facility is located below the levee on a tree-shaded berm where there's space for parking.

Three miles farther is Clarksburg. A water-borne expedition led by Father Narcisco Duran is believed to have camped here in 1817. Shaded by 3,000 black walnut trees, Clarksburg is a pleasant town where housewives grow giant pumpkins in their backyards to raise funds for such causes as the Clarksburg Chapter of the Future Farmers of America. The town is supported by the American Crystal Sugar Refinery, a blend of modern machinery and antique buildings, which abuts the South River Road.

Clarksburg was settled in 1849 by Judge Robert Clark who planted the first peach orchard in Yolo County. Such was the marshy character of the land that Isaac P. Parson found most of the farmers living on houseboats when he arrived at Clarksburg in 1911 to buy acreage for the Netherlands Farms Company.

Clarksburg has a marina and farther up the South River Road are Mal's Garcia Bend Landing, Austen's Brickyard Marina, and Sherwood Harbor at Chicory Bend.

For a look at the countryside and the Sacramento Ship Channel, we turn left just north of town on the Pumphouse Road. This levee road follows Winchester Slough, an excellent black bass water. At one point, the road crosses the Holland Branch of the Sacramento Northern Railroad which terminates at lonely

Oxford Station on Prospect Island. Such feeder lines contributed greatly to the decline of the river trade.

Among the crops we see on this drive is corn. California isn't a corn state. But, of twenty outstanding production records in the United States, a total of six were achieved in the Clarksburg area with yields of 185 to 219 bushels an acre. The combination of good soil, humid air, warm sunny days, and moderately cool nights has proved perfect for corn as well as sugar beets.

Another crop much in evidence around Clarksburg is alfalfa. A native of southern Europe, alfalfa was known as "Chile clover" when it was imported to California in 1855. The first successful crop in Yolo County was grown by Nicholas Wyckoff in 1870. Now the No. 1 field crop in California, alfalfa, grown in rotation with corn, tomatoes, or sugar beets, has the advantage of restoring nitrogen to the soil.

Three miles from the river, we turn north on Jefferson Boulevard and proceed a mile or so to a parking area which overlooks the Sacramento Ship Channel. This is one of the few waterways in the Delta without a perceptible current. Across the channel is a broad depression known as the Yolo Bypass. This trough floods in high water years and thereby serves to relieve some of the pressure exerted on the river dikes. It was constructed about the time the Netherlands Farms Company reclaimed the Clarksburg area. Farmers lease land in the Yolo Bypass to grow hay and grain on its rich bottomland in dry years. Pheasant shooting is good along the bypass, but public access is limited. Information about the area may be obtained from sporting goods stores in Sacramento.

From the parking area, Jefferson Boulevard bears northeast five miles to the Sacramento Barge Lock in West Sacramento. The lock is required because the water in the Port of Sacramento is twelve feet lower than the main river. There's an observation platform near the bascule bridge which spans the barge canal where you may watch barges and pleasure boats pass through the lock.

Across the bridge, Stone Boulevard leads west from Jefferson Boulevard to approach the port where there are berths for five deep-draft vessels. The port was in the planning stages as early as 1911 but politics, wars, and depressions delayed construction, so it wasn't completed until 1963. Exports include rice, canned goods, and timber. There are guided tours of the port on Sunday afternoons from 12:30 to 4:30. The tours begin at the port entrance on Harbor Boulevard.

Jefferson Boulevard continues to an interchange for the Sacramento Freeway. Two blocks farther, the boulevard terminates at West Capitol Avenue where there are restaurants, shopping centers, and scores of motels and motor lodges.

8 THE SACRAMENTO WATERFRONT

"Rivers dominated the valley scene for about twenty years before encountering opposition from railroads. They were the highways over which moved all freight and most of the passengers. It was along their banks that the first commercial towns, the first cultural centers, and the first county seats were located."

HISTORY OF THE SACRAMENTO VALLEY
by Joseph A. McGowan, 1961

Sacramento's deep water port is filled with interest, but for excitement it may never compare with the old waterfront where the paddlewheel steamers used to dock. This was the embarcadero for Sutter's Fort until 1848 when the debt-ridden Sutter gave the frontage to his son to avoid foreclosure. Against his father's wishes, John Sutter, Jr., laid out a city here which mushroomed in 1849 from two log cabins to more than 100 buildings.

In the frenzy of the Gold Rush, the town was a raw, ramshackle settlement crowded with bars, brothels, and gambling halls. The river off the embarcadero was jammed with sailing vessels deserted by their crews for the Mother Lode. Somehow, this shabby port survived fires, floods, riots, and pestilence to emerge in a few years time as the state capitol and premier trading center of the Sacramento Valley.

Because of its central location, Sacramento was bound to prosper as a hub for road and rail traffic. But it was the river trade which put the city on the map and made fortunes for the pioneer merchants engaged in supplying the Mother Lode.

In 1854, rival steamers on the river merged to form the Cali-

Weekend traffic on the Sacramento River.

fornia Steam Navigation Company. Thereafter, freight rates for goods delivered from San Francisco were boosted to as much as 50% of the purchase price. Sacramento merchants screamed charges of "monopoly," although few were badly hurt because their customary mark-up ran as high as 200% of the San Francisco price.

Old Sacramento attained elegance in the 1850's, but, a century later, it was a decaying skid row full of cheap flop houses. The business district had moved away from the waterfront and proponents of redevelopment were pushing plans to demolish the old quarter down to the last brick. The "progressives" disdained the "reactionaries" who argued the eight block area bound by Front, Third, I, and L Streets contained more buildings of historic interest than any other city in California.

The issue was joined when it was announced the new Interstate 5 freeway would preempt the old town. Historians pleaded in vain for the freeway to be routed on the west bank of the river but finally achieved a compromise whereby four blocks encompassing 26 acres would be saved. It was decided part of this frontage would be reconstructed for a state park, leaving the remainder for private investors to develop as restaurants, antique shops, and such.

The most convenient approach to Old Sacramento is the pedestrian underpass which leaves the parking area at the K Street shopping mall. Reconstruction is expected to take years but already some buildings have been restored. These include the B. F. Hasting's Bank Building (1853) which was the western terminous for the Pony Express. Rebuilt on a new site after it was torn down for the freeway is the "Big Four" building (1852) where the merchants Crocker, Hastings, Huntington, and Stanford hatched plans for a transcontinental railway.

One of the saddest sights on the river is the old *Delta King* mouldering at the foot of the Capitol Mall. Hopefully, this paddle-

The "Delta Queen." Together with the "Delta King" these paddlewheel steamers made daily runs between San Francisco and Sacramento in the years 1926 thru 1941. The "Delta Queen" now plys the Ohio and Mississippi Rivers as an excursion boat.

wheel steamer will be restored and made a permanent addition to Old Sacramento. The sister ship, *Delta Queen*, presently plies the Mississippi River on extended cruises. From 1926 until 1941, the *Delta King* and *Delta Queen* provided daily overnight passenger service between the capitol and San Francisco. In 1939, the fare was $1.50 one way, $1.95 round trip, and $3.50 to $5.00 for a stateroom with twin beds and a bath or shower.

Prefabricated in Scotland, the *Delta King* and *Delta Queen* were the largest, fastest, stern-wheelers ever to navigate the Delta. Each was 250 feet long and of 1,837 gross tons, with 2,000 h.p. compound engines. For luxury, they were equipped in the tradition of such earlier "floating palaces" as the *Senator,* the *New World,* and the lovely *Chrysopolis.* The food was superb and there was music for dancing in the social hall which was roofed by a dome of stained glass hung with crystal chandeliers.

The caretaker of the *Delta King* sometimes permits visitors to inspect the vessel on Sundays. After service as a military ferry in World War II, the ship provided steam heat for a hospital in British Columbia. Later, it was berthed at Stockton as a floating barracks for field workers. Just how the *Delta King* ended up at Sacramento is something of a mystery. Rumor has it the vessel was "pirated" from Stockton by a Sacramento group dedicated to the preservation of New Orleans jazz music.

Across the river from Old Sacramento is Broderick which was recently alleged to have the worst "sub-standard housing" in Yolo County. First known as Washington, in 1864 it became the site of the first salmon cannery in the world.

North from Eye Street by way of Jibboom Street, we approach Discovery Park located at the confluence of the American and Sacramento Rivers. This attractive fishing access was the site of a shanty town in the depression of the 1930's. First opened in 1964, the park has a six-lane boat ramp and affords four miles of bank fishing. The American River Hiking and Riding Trail begins here. A short distance up the Garden Highway from Discovery Park is the Village Marina which has boat rentals and vehicle camping.

Trolling and anchor fishing at the mouth of the American River is apt to be best for fall-run salmon from early July through September and for spring-run fish from late November through February. Striped bass fishing peaks in early spring. Shad are taken in June and July.

Another waterfront recreation area is Miller Park at the foot of Broadway. There is a marina and public boat ramp located here.

It's beyond the scope of this guidebook to cover the many points of interest in Sacramento which are removed from the waterfront. But, to mention a few places, there's Sutter's Fort, the State Indian Museum, the Crocker Art Gallery, William Land Park and Zoo, State Library, and the Capitol Park which contains 40,000 different varieties of trees, shrubs, and flowers.

9 THE RIVER ROAD

"Stately Victorian mansions lie behind the levees; their intricate fish scale shingles the work of artisans of another era. The houses are often several stories high; it was cooler that way in pre-airconditioning days. The tall buildings served another practical purpose. Over the years, people have waited on these upper floors for the flood rescue boats. These old homes have known the taste of river water and survived."

SAN MATEO TIMES by Mary Jane Clinton, 1972

South from the Capitol Mall to city limits, there are no thoroughfares in Sacramento which afford a view of the waterfront. Riverside Drive leaves Broadway to approach Green's Brickyard, Light 29, and other resort landings, but this street runs below the levee. From the Capitol Park, it's nine miles by way of Fifteenth Street and Freeport Boulevard to Freeport where State Route 160 first meets the river and becomes a levee road.

The River Road south to Walnut Grove was made a public highway in 1863.

Now a hamlet, Freeport was founded in 1862 by the Freeport Railroad Company who hoped the town might overtake Sacramento. The idea was to bypass the capitol with a line that would join the Sacramento Valley Railroad at a point halfway between Sacramento and Folsom. Freeport was literally a "free port" in the sense no tax was charged for goods "in transit" as was the case at Sacramento. Nine miles of track were laid before the railroad failed.

The early settlers at Freeport included commercial fishermen of Portuguese descent who lived on the river in houseboats. These hardy "river rats" were reported to shoot at steamers

A remnant of the past at Courtland.
Present 600 population is predominantly Chicano.

which strayed too close to their nets. Such incidents were common off Collinsville until the steamer captains elected to return the fire with shotguns.

The Freeport Marina has bait, boat rentals, and a park for house trailers. One mile south of Freeport is Cliff's Place, a landing with boat rentals and overnight accommodations.

Seven miles farther is Hood. On the drive to Hood, we pass some elegant Victorian farmhouses and numerous pear orchards.

The Delta is the oldest of five pear growing areas in California. Some orchards on the islands have trees over a hundred years old. It was in the 1870's many farmers who couldn't break even growing 1,000 acres of wheat discovered they could live in style on less than 50 acres of fruit trees. Rail shipments of pears to Eastern markets began years before the first refrigerator cars became operational in 1888. Pears were found to be the fruit most suitable for cultivation in the Delta, partly because they are tolerant of wet soil.

All pears grown commercially in the Delta are Bartletts, a variety perfected by the English schoolmaster, John Stair, in 1770. The Delta crop is harvested in July, at which time the trailer cities of orchard workers are seen in the fields. As yet, no machines have been devised which can perform the work of picking, sorting, and grading pears. In a good year, the Delta produces up to 90,000 tons of fruit, but the crop is highly vulnerable to frost, hail, wind, blight, insects, and excessive heat. Lately, some Delta orchardists have obtained good results using natural insect predators instead of chemical pesticides.

Hood (population 330) is a shipping point for pears on the railroad which runs to Isleton. It was named in 1910 for William Hood who was chief engineer of the Southern Pacific.

About 1½ miles south of Hood, the road leaves the levee to skirt Randall Island. We return to the levee just before Courtland, which was founded in the 1860's by James V. Sims. After a stint in the mines, Sims turned farmer and was among the first to grow grapes commercially in California.

Courtland had several fish canneries and a large Chinese community in the early days. The Chinese were reported about to open a clothing factory when their settlement burned in December 1879. The population today (about 600) is mostly Chicano, but some dwellings in the old quarter still bear Chinese symbols.

Lincoln Chan, one of the largest independent growers in the Delta, maintains a machine shop and farm implement center at Courtland. Not long ago, the volunteer fire department created a mild sensation when it recruited 25-year-old Sally Hearne as a fire fighter.

The Courtland Dock has a restaurant and boat rentals. On the south side of town near the Paintersville Bridge was the site of a store, saloon, and hotel built by Levi Painter in 1852. Painter became famous on the river for his "post hole bank." On moonless nights, Painter would bury money left with him for safekeeping beneath one of the many fence posts which enclosed his property.

Today, the site of Paintersville is occupied by J. M. Buckley and Sons, a trucking firm established in 1918. The railroads cut deeply into the river trade, but it was the combination of trucks and improved roads which rang down the curtain on paddle-wheel navigation.

Hundreds of small landings on the Sacramento faded away after the passing of the steamers. The nautical chart 5828-SC (Andrus Island to Sacramento) shows the sites of many vanished landings. The principal landings had wharves but there were also scores of "brush landings" where a steamer would lay its gangplank on a heap of fruit tree prunings or other debris piled on the levee.

When a farmer wanted a steamboat to stop at his landing, he

Bait fishing off the levee near Freeport.

hung out a flag by day or a lantern by night. Often the steamers were called to stop for no more than a sack of potatoes. On one run, the *Isleton* made 46 stops between San Francisco and Sacramento and 76 stops on the return trip. When the steamship companies ordered their vessels not to stop for less than $1.25 worth of business, the disgruntled farmers turned to the trucking outfits.

Among the steamers which sparked excitement at the landings were the *Sentinel* and the *Weitchpec*. These were floating department stores where farmers who lacked ready cash could trade such items as a bushel of beans or a live pig for merchandise.

Across the river from Paintersville, the streets of Onisbo were surveyed in 1849. This "paper city" lost its post office to Courtland sometime in the 1860's.

IO THE MEADOWS

"Even the most remote sloughs, including those which surround such a well known spot as The Meadows, are affected by the tides. It has become a sight all too common to find some hapless boating party, particularly those in a flat bottomed houseboat, stuck on a sandbar, because they have become too intent upon catching those big 'uns."

THE SACRAMENTO BEE by Dorothy Augusta, 1970

The Meadows Area east of Walnut Grove is a lovely everglade — a half wild place of tule marsh and quiet tree-shaded waterways covered with pond lilies and water hyacinths. Here on Snodgrass Slough, Lost Slough, and the Meadows Slough are favorite overnight anchorages for cruisers and houseboats.

The Army Engineers' standards for levee maintenance were never fully implemented in the Meadows, apparently because the property owners took a forceful stand against cutting the trees. In recent years, the state has been making appraisals of land in the area for a future state park.

The heart of the Meadows is most easily explored in a boat. However, some of the area's charms may be glimpsed on the Twin Cities Road which leaves the River Road about seven miles south of Courtland. From the turn-off, it's two miles to a swing bridge on beautiful Snodgrass Slough. This is fine water for sunfish, crappie, and largemouth black bass.

Snodgrass has yielded largemouth to 11½ pounds and the record white catfish for California which weighed 15 pounds, 1 ounce. Favorite bass lures on the slough include rubber worms, surface plugs, diving lures, and live minnows. Lines with a breaking strength of no less than 10 pound test are recommended because the productive water is thick with snags and aquatic plants.

We continue east on the Twin Cities Road through lush fields grazed by sheep and cattle. Four miles from Snodgrass Slough, we turn south on Thornton Road and proceed three miles to the Benson Ferry Bridge. This swing bridge spans the Mokelumne River just below its confluence with the Consumnes River. A ferry established here in 1849 was purchased in 1850 by John A. Benson who built the principal wagon road between Sacramento and Stockton.

About one-third of a mile east of the bridge, Mokelumne City was founded in 1854. The settlement grew rapidly and seemed to have a bright future before it was washed out by the flood of 1862. In this year, Dr. D. L. Locke formed the Mokelumne Steam Navigation Company to serve Lockeford which lies 22 miles upriver east of Lodi. The steamers *Pert* and *O.K.* were able to navigate this far until 1864.

Across the Benson Ferry Bridge, we enter San Joaquin County. It's two miles to Thornton, a sleepy crossroads supported by Plant No. 6 of the California Canners & Growers. Here, in 1855, Arthur Thornton founded New Hope Ranch. The name was changed to Thornton when the Western Pacific laid track across the ranch in 1907.

At Thornton, we turn west on the Walnut Grove Road and proceed four miles to the swing bridge which spans the South Branch of the Mokelumne River at New Hope Landing. The river forks just above the landing. There are three marinas at New Hope with a motel, stores, restaurants, and grounds for tent and vehicle camping. Fishing skiffs, runabouts for water skiing, and houseboats may be rented.

Delta liveries rent three kinds of houseboats. The so-called "picnic barge" is only for day use. The catamaran houseboat — a modified house trailer mounted on pontoons — is powered by an outboard motor. Its maximum speed rarely exceeds 12 m.p.h. Much faster and easier to navigate is the houseboat cruiser, which has a steel hull and single or twin inboard engines.

Both types of houseboats, ranging 30 to 50 feet in length, come equipped with a stove, dinette, refrigerator, sleeping bunks, closets, and a lavatory. Some of the larger craft which sleep eight to ten people have separate bedrooms with stall showers.

Rentals range from $300 to $500 a week in the summer season; from $225 to $350 in the "off season." The daily rate for the smallest catamaran sleeping four people may run as low as $50 in summer. Deposits of $50 to $300 are required and gasoline is not covered in the rental fee. The boats have dishes, cooking utensils and such. Blankets, linens, and towels are not supplied.

Such is the popularity of houseboating in the Delta that reservations for summer must be booked months in advance. Most liveries provide a map and some instruction in navigation. Docking a houseboat takes a little know-how and all boat operators are expected to be familiar with the rules of the road as outlined in the "ABC's of California Boating Law." Another useful pamphlet is "Safe Boating on the Sacramento River" published by the Department of Navigation and Ocean Development.

Critical to the success of a houseboat trip is the selection of a safe overnight anchorage where sleepers will not be disturbed by the traffic of passing boats or wake up to find themselves stranded on a mud flat. The locations of many good anchorages are shown on the "Weekend Outdoor Map" available at most marinas and bait stores.

Bridge clearances are shown on the "Delta Region Map" published by the Delta Marina Yacht Harbor at Rio Vista. Most houseboats require a clearance of at least eleven feet.

New Hope Landing on the Mokelumne River.

Two annuals packed with information on Delta waterways are Sunset's "Where to Go Boating in California" and Captain Berssen's Northern California edition of the "Boating and Fishing Almanac." The full spectrum of Delta boating activity is covered in the "Bay and Delta Yachtsman" published monthly at Rio Vista. The guidebook, "Delta Country," was written by Ron and Peggy Miller especially for houseboat enthusiasts. A must for extended trips by houseboat or cruiser are the nautical charts of the U. S. Coast and Geodetic Survey. These are listed in the bibliography.

From the New Hope Bridge, we cross the tip of Staten Island to the Miller's Ferry Bridge. On this span, we pass to Tyler Island, one of several tracts in the Delta where wheat is still grown in quantity.

Up through the 1870's, wheat was king in the Delta with fabulous yields of 60 to 70 bushels to an acre. Thereafter, production dropped because of competition from other growing areas and exhaustion of the soil. Around 1900, many wheat farmers switched to barley, a late winter crop' mostly used for cattle feed.

With a growing world market for grain, there's talk wheat might make a comeback in the Delta. But a Tyler Island farmer interviewed by Terry Burnham of the Sacramento Bee described the cost of raising wheat as "frighteningly high." In 1972, the average cost in the Delta was estimated at about $120 an acre against a gross income of $170 an acre. Although wheat enjoys a federal subsidy, the farmer must establish a production record to qualify.

Just over the Miller's Ferry Bridge, we turn right on the levee to Guisti's, a country style Italian restaurant which was one of Erle Stanley Gardner's favorite places. Reservations may be required several days in advance to obtain a table here on weekends.

A little farther on the levee opposite Dead Horse Island is the Walnut Grove Marina, otherwise known as "The Gateway to the Meadows." This large establishment has houseboats for rent.

Shortly, the road comes out on Georgiana Slough where Jack London spent some summers on his boat. London would begin each day by writing 1,500 words and then take off on foot to visit friends in Walnut Grove.

Georgiana Slough winds fifteen miles from the Sacramento to the lower Mokelumne River. Despite many twists and turns and numerous snags, the slough was traveled by steamers which provided regular freight and passenger service between Stockton and Sacramento. The trip was 60 miles, except during floods when the steamers would cut across the islands. This was known as "wheatfield navigation."

II WALNUT GROVE AND LOCKE

"One of the persistent themes in the history of the Sacramento Valley and the state as a whole has been nativism, a philosophy or attitude which held that Anglo-Saxons were entitled to the first fruits of the land and other groups should be content with the left-overs."

THE HISTORY OF THE SACRAMENTO VALLEY
by Joseph A. McGowan, 1961

Walnut Grove is a quiet farm center where campers and house-boat parties visit to stock up on groceries. The markets here and next door at Locke are operated by Chinese-Americans descended from the "China King," who was among the first Chinese to settle in the Delta. The Fruit Exchange has a shipping yard at Walnut Grove as does Lum Bunn Fong, a large independent grower and packer.

The site of Walnut Grove was settled by John W. Sharp in 1851. A sawmill operated in the years 1865-75 and, thereafter, the town thrived as a steamer landing for produce.

In the early years, Walnut Grove was reputed to be a hangout for bandits. The lore of the Delta includes tales of river pirates stretching chains across the waterways to snag steamboats laden with gold. But no documents have been found to verify such incidents.

The Chinese quarter at Walnut Grove burned in 1915 and again in 1937. What remains of the old quarter at the north end of town affords the bleak aspect of a decaying rural slum. Many of the weathered stores and dwellings are vacant.

The village of Locke is separated from Walnut Grove by the Delta Cross Channel which links the Sacramento River with Snodgrass Slough. Fishing skiffs (but not houseboats) may

Old quarter at Walnut Grove.

use the channel when the gate is raised. Water is drawn through the channel and across the Delta by giant pumps situated near Tracy. One set of pumps serves the Central Valley Project and another the State Water Project.

The Delta Cross Channel is spanned by one of the few fixed bridges in the Delta. Off the River Road near the north bank of the channel rises the tallest structure in California—a television tower which crests at 1,549 feet.

On the river side of the levee is a huge packing shed where paddlewheel steamers loaded produce. The shed is presently used to store pleasure boats. We park near the shed and walk behind the levee to discover the only rural Chinese village in the United States.

The narrow main street of Locke is lined with rickety 2-3 story wood frame buildings, fronted by balconies which lean over the sidewalks. Except for the Chinese lettering on the stores, the village might pass for a frontier town of the Old West.

Actually, Locke isn't very old. There were only a few houses before the 1915 fire at Walnut Grove caused many Chinese families to relocate here. Then the population swelled to 1,500 and the town acquired fish markets, herb stores, dry goods emporiums, ten boarding houses, a hotel, and the Star Theatre at which Chinese opera was performed.

Both Locke and Walnut Grove were wide-open towns in the 1920's and 1930's, where thousands of field workers—mostly single men from Mexico and the Philippines—found momentary escape from their harsh conditions of life at speakeasies, brothels, gambling rooms, and secret opium dens.

The Delta once contained many Chinese settlements, most of which were obliterated by fire or flood before the turn of the century. Forced out of the diggings by threats of violence from Caucasian miners, a few Chinese arrived in the Delta as early as 1850. Some worked on the dikes with resident Indians and

Of the many towns founded by Chinese in the Delta,
only Locke remains. Other settlements were
destroyed by fire and flood.

Kanakas from Hawaii. Almost all the Delta ranches acquired Chinese cooks who labored from dawn to dusk scrubbing clothes when they weren't tending the stove.

A great influx of Chinese into the Delta occurred in 1869-70 after the transcontinental railway was joined and the Central Pacific laid off 12,000 laborers. In the 1870's, all-Chinese crews were employed building the levees, for which they were paid 13½ cents a cubic yard. The laborers were represented in their dealings with the landowners by contractors, such as the "China King," who could speak English.

The work gangs were gradually displaced by clamshell dredgers which could move as much earth in a day as 500 men with shovels and wheelbarrows and for as little as 4 cents a cubic yard.

Mechanization came early to the big wheat ranches of the Delta. Few had jobs for the displaced laborers, but many Chinese used their savings to rent plots on the islands where they grew melons, sweet potatoes, cucumbers, squash, peanuts, celery, and leaf vegetables. Apparently, salads were unknown in the West before Chinese produce entered the market. As late as the 1860's, it was not unusual to hear salad greens denounced as "cow feed." It was from Chinese and later Italian and Japanese truck gardeners the landowners learned diversified farming.

Thousands of Chinese found work in the fields when the big ranches switched to growing crops such as corn and beans which required much hand labor. But, at this time during the depression years of the late 1870's, white workers in the cities were mobilized by Denis Kearney to demand, "The Chinese must go!" Secret societies, such as the "Order of Caucasians," instigated lynching parties and set many Chinese settlements on fire. One result was a decision by Congress in 1882 to ban further immigration from China.

But, a few years following the Chinese Exclusion Act, the big growers turned to recruiting laborers from Japan who underbid the Chinese by agreeing to work for as little as 35 cents a day. There was a movement of Chinese to the cities although many lingered in the Delta to till the islands as tenant farmers. In 1915, 75% of the Delta was cultivated by tenant farmers of whom 76% were reported to be Oriental.

The post office at Locke closed a few years ago and today the population numbers less than 75 Chinese families plus a few residents of different ancestry. Most of the Chinese are elderly retired people, the younger generation having left to enter business and professions. Of late, some Caucasians have moved in to open craft shops and restaurants, such as the Tule Cafe which serves beer and pizza.

Locke is situated on the Locke Ranch, part of a huge estate for which the heirs of Nell and Alice Locke must pay $200,000 in probate fees and inheritance taxes. To raise this money, some heirs want to sell the land and some don't. A suit has been filed in Sacramento Superior Court asking the land be partitioned among all the heirs. So it appears Locke's future largely depends on which heir is awarded the town.

12 ANDRUS ISLAND

"ISLETON — Mayor M. J. 'Butch' Franscioni's troubles started last week when he mangled his left hand in a harvester while working on his 226 acre ranch just outside of town. Yesterday the 72 year old mayor lost the harvester, his entire ranch, and very nearly his entire town to the swollen flood waters of the San Joaquin River."

THE SAN FRANCISCO EXAMINER by Don Martinez, 1972

It may be years before Andrus Island completely recovers from the flood which caused $22 million damage to 16 resorts, 77 farms, and scores of dwellings in the town of Isleton following a levee break on the night of June 20, 1971. Of more than 100 levee breaks since 1900, this was among the worst because it occurred on the most populated island in the Delta.

From a small gap in the levee which fronts the San Joaquin River, a five-foot wall of water fanned out across Andrus Island, forcing a hasty evacuation of 3,000 residents and resort guests. On the morning of June 21, the flood spilled over the low dikes which enclose Jackson Slough to inundate farms on neighboring Brannan Island.

Air Force helicopters and vessels of the Coast Guard were called in to rescue families stranded on the roofs of some isolated ranches. But there were no fatalities and few people required hospitalization. Within six weeks, some resorts were back in business. Hardest hit were the farmers who had to wait eight months for pumps to remove 58 billion gallons of water from thirty square miles of fields and orchards.

Andrus Island was settled by George Andrus in 1852. The tract was flooded often after it was first reclaimed in the 1860's but the 1972 flood was only the second time the dikes have failed in the present century.

From Walnut Grove, we cross a swing bridge on Georgiana Slough to the northern panhandle of Andrus Island. The pear orchards here stayed dry in the 1972 flood, thanks to an interior levee which divides the panhandle from the lower island.

On the two mile drive along the River Road to Greening's Ko-ket Resort, we pass numerous sidings where bank fishermen gather. Greening's has sites on the levee for tent and vehicle camping. Four miles south of Greening's, the road affords a view of Andrus Island where it was covered with fourteen feet of water. Three miles farther is Isleton (population 1,300) which is the largest town in the Delta.

Isleton was founded in 1874 by Josiah Pool, a veteran of the Mexican War. Just previous to the flood of 1881, the settlement boasted a wharf, hotel, post office, two stores, and a small plant which attempted to refine sugar from watermelons. In the 1920's, Isleton was just as riproaring a town as Locke or Walnut Grove. It had several asparagus canneries and people came from miles around to enjoy an evening in "The Little Paris of the Delta."

The main street of Isleton occupies some of the highest ground on Andrus Island. The shops here were forced to close during the 1972 flood only because the water and sewage systems failed. At one end of town are some attractive new buildings, including a library, branch bank, post office, and church. However, much of the business district is old and delapidated.

Isleton had no physician for several years previous to the arrival of Dr. James Rushing early in 1972. Rushing was assigned to the town by the National Health Service Corps under a federal program intended to provide medical service to remote communities.

The levee break in 1972 occurred at a point four miles due south of Isleton. Word of the break was relayed by the lone night

Bumpnetting for spring-run shad on the Mokelumne River. The action is best from dusk to midnight.

operator of the General Telephone Company at Courtland several hours before the flood waters reached the edge of Isleton. There was time for Colonel James Donovan of the Army Engineers to recruit a fleet of trucks and tractors with which to throw up an emergency dike around the town. Hundreds of volunteers helped state and federal employees pile sand bags on the dike. But on the evening of June 22, the dike suddenly gave way forcing the workers to run for their lives.

On June 27, President Nixon declared Andrus and Brannan Islands a disaster area, thereby paving the way for release of $24.5 million in relief funds requested by Governor Reagan. This aid included help for 800 farm workers and townspeople who lost not only their homes but up to a full year of employment.

We continue south on the River Road one mile to a small wooded berm known as Ida Island. Here is Vierra's Resort which has a restaurant, boat rentals, cottages, and tent and vehicle camping. Two miles farther is the Cliffhouse Public Fishing Access with parking space for bank fishermen. Next door, the Cliffhouse Resort has launching and boat rentals.

Another mile brings us to the Rio Vista Bridge where we turn east on State Highway 12 and proceed 3½ miles to an intersection with the Jackson Slough Road. Two miles south on this road, we come out on the levee at Seven Mile Slough. A mile east on the levee is Bruno's Yacht Harbor, one of the relatively few Delta marinas which provide moorage for sailing craft.

Bruno's is situated near the site of the 1972 levee break. Just up the road where Seven Mile Slough opens to the main channel of the San Joaquin, the attractive new Spindrift Resort was totally destroyed by the flood. Expensive cruisers and sailing yachts were torn from their moorings at Spindrift and smashed into kindling.

It's believed the break originated from a slight seepage at one small spot on the levee. This is how most dike failures in the

Delta begin. If the seepage had occurred during the day, it surely would have been noticed in time for a maintenance crew to effect repairs. But it was past midnight when two sheriff's deputies on routine patrol discovered the river pouring through a gap that was twenty feet wide. After radioing for help, the deputies switched on the siren of their patrol car.

Bill Partington and his wife in a trailer park near Spindrift heard the siren just in time for them to struggle through chest-high water for the safety of the levee. Sleeping at Spindrift aboard their 37-foot houseboat, Mr. and Mrs. Clarence Kentch of Los Angeles were less fortunate. They suffered a bruising ride inland to a cornfield where a helicopter found them at dawn. One evacuee reported the inrushing water sounded like "the roar of thunder."

Oddly, the flood occurred in a "dry year" when the run-off from the Sierra was the lowest in a decade. The authorities speculated that a high tide and 45 m.p.h. winds had undermined a portion of the levee which had been weakened by muskrat tunnels. A maintenance crew had been working on the levee just previous to the flood and there was talk a bulldozer might have damaged the foundations. Some Delta residents pointed an accusing finger at the Army Engineers for removal of the trees.

But however much local opinion is divided on the cause of the Andrus Island disaster, everyone agrees that most privately owned dikes are growing old. All receive careful maintenance, but, in many cases, the funds are lacking for a complete structural overhaul such as the Army Engineers performed on the Sacramento River dikes.

Presently, the islands are sinking beneath the weight of levees as much as 2-3 inches a year. And mounting recreational use of the Delta has created problems. The dikes are made vulnerable to erosion by bank fishermen who park on the soft sidings of levee roads. Much wear and tear on the levees is

Bruno's Yacht Harbor on Seven Mile Slough.
The marina was one of 16 resorts destroyed or
severely damaged when Andrus Island was
flooded in June 1972.

caused by pleasure boats traveling at high speeds. Such traffic required 25 miles of levees on Staten Island to be faced with rock several times in recent years. Rocking costs $10 a lineal foot and the entire expense is borne by the landowners.

The cost of levee maintenance, rising taxes, and competition from growers outside the Delta caused the owners of 983-acre Quimby Island to propose a multi-million dollar recreational development. In place of the farms on Quimby Island, they would substitute lagoons and floating clubhouses. Some observers fear the entire Delta may go this way, notwithstanding its importance as one of the most fertile growing areas in the world.

A few months after the Andrus Island levee break, John Teerink told the California Water Commission that it might be a good idea not to reclaim tracts which became flooded. Instead, he suggested they be set aside as wildlife refuges and places of recreation. When Isleton's Mayor "Butch" Fransciosi was asked what he thought of Teerink's proposal, the 72-year-old farmer replied, "I think the man should be locked up!"

However, Teerink's concern as deputy director of the Water Resources Department is to obtain more high quality water for delivery to Southern California by way of the California Aqueduct. If farming was phased out in the Delta, there might be less opposition to such projects as the $200 million Peripheral Canal which would divert water from the Sacramento above the Delta. Critics charge the project would lower the water quality of the Delta and aggravate pollution in San Francisco Bay.

The levee break on Andrus Island grew to 900 feet wide before repair crews could begin work on it. The inrushing water swept away the peat foundation, leaving a cavity which extended 75 feet down to a sub-stratum of clay. This clay was formed eons ago when the Central Valley was an inland sea. Five weeks were required to fill the break with barge-loads of rock and thousands of tons of river silt collected by suction dredges.

Along the Andrus Island levee east of Bruno's, we find numerous resort landings. Most of these are large establishments offering a wide range of facilities. First is the San Andreas Boat Harbor, named for the San Andreas Shoal which is one of the best places to fish for catfish and striped bass on the lower San Joaquin. Trolling is a popular way to catch stripers on the shoals in early spring. The favorite offering is a bugeye jig and red-and-white plug trolled in tandem on a wire spreader rig.

Two miles farther east is Happy Harbor which has a trailer park. Next on the wooded point where the Mokelumne River enters the San Joaquin is Korth's Pirate Lair, one of the oldest, most beautiful resorts in the Delta. Korth's includes a motel and camping in the shade of conifers and eucalyptus.

Driving north up the levee which fronts the Mokelumne, we come to Moore's Riverboat Yacht Haven which has houseboats for rent and a popular restaurant converted from an old river steamer.

Then follows Willow Berm Harbor, The Lighthouse Resort (houseboat rentals), Rancho Marina, Sycamore Park, and Perry's Dry Dock and Yacht Harbor. The last resort is the B&W Harbor where houseboats are both sold and rented. The B&W includes a restaurant, camping, and attractive lodge-type accommodations.

Upriver from the B&W Harbor is favorite water for "bump netting," a local method of night fishing for spring-run American shad. A homemade net of chicken wire with an eight-foot handle is held in two feet of water off the stern of a slow-moving skiff. The outboard motor is tilted to create a turbulence on the surface which attracts the fish. When the fisherman feels a shad bump the net, he heaves the fish aboard. The action usually peaks in May.

American shad were the first game fish introduced to California waters from outside the state. Ten thousand baby shad delivered by rail from New York were released into the Sacramento River by the pioneer fish culturist, Seth Green, in 1871. Thereafter in the Seventies, white catfish, black bass, and striped bass were successfully stocked. Aside from the migratory salmon, steelhead, and sturgeon, the only game fish found in the Delta at the time of the Gold Rush was the Sacramento perch. Now scarce in California waters, these sunfish abound in Nevada's Walker and Pyramid Lakes.

Shad contain something like 860 bones but they are delicious smoked or baked in a very slow oven so that all but the largest bones are dissolved. Light tackle with wet flies and tiny flashbaits are used to take shad in the American River upstream from Discovery Park.

Venice Island Ferry.

13 TERMINOUS, KING ISLAND, AND THE EMPIRE TRACT

"At first I rowed myself to school. However, later when the region became more inhabited, speedboats picked up the children. The schoolhouse was on an island then called Cattlemen's Ranch and now known as the Empire Tract. There weren't too many pupils—mostly the children of Japanese and Chinese farm workers. Some days I'd be the only one in class!"

THE SAN FRANCISCO CHRONICLE
by Hyress Scarlett as told to Millie Robbins, 1967

California Highway 12 leaves Andrus Island near the B&W Boat Harbor on a swing bridge which spans the Mokelumne River to Bouldin Island. Midway across the bridge is the Sacramento-San Joaquin County line. East from the bridge, the highway cuts across the cultivated interior of Bouldin Island where the traveler may encounter clouds of choking peat dust in summer.

In the 1870's Bouldin Island was owned by the Pacific Distillery Company of San Francisco. At this time, most of the tract's 6,500 acres were given over to grain and potatoes. Later, some time in the 1880's, beds of asparagus were planted and, in 1892, Robert Hickman built on "Boulder Island" the first asparagus cannery in the United States.

About two miles east from the bridge crossing, a road leaves north for Mary's Boat House on the South Fork of the Mokelumne. Four miles farther on the main highway, we cross Little Potato Slough to Terminous.

In 1900, John Dougherty built a road out of Lodi which terminated where Little Potato Slough joins the Mokelumne South Fork. The barge landing at the roadhead became known as Terminous instead of Terminus because somebody goofed when

85

the settlement applied for a post office. Terminous rose to prominence as a shipping point for produce after the Western Pacific Railroad ran a line to it in 1907. In the peak years, as many as 2,500 laborers lived at Terminous in a "box car city" behind the levee.

Rail service to Terminous ended in 1961. All that remains of the old shipping facility are three warehouses used to store pleasure boats. Terminous is now a resort landing which claims the largest marina in the Delta. The Tower Park Marina and Resort has a restaurant, fishing skiffs and houseboats for rent, and both tent and vehicle camping. On the north side of the bridge is the landing for the Staten Island public ferry. Near the ferry landing is Bayport-on-the-Delta, a marina with boat rentals and overnight accommodations.

Above Terminous, three quiet dead-end sloughs branch east from the South Fork of the Mokelumne. These are Hog Slough, Beaver Slough, and Sycamore Slough. There isn't better water in the Delta to fish for brown bullhead, black bullhead, crappie, largemouth bass, and "sunnies," such as warmouth and blue-gill. March, April, and May are the most productive months for bass and catfish.

Six miles east of Terminous, we turn south on the Thornton Road and proceed five miles to an intersection with the Eight Mile Road. The latter road crosses the Cohn Tract to Bishop Cut. Just south of the Cohn Tract across Disappointment Slough is the Shima Tract, named for George Shima, "The Potato King of the World."

Shima was among the thousands of Japanese recruited by the big growers after immigration from China was halted and the resident Chinese began to demand better wages and working conditions. Despite pitifully low pay, it wasn't long before some Japanese acquired their own farms in the Delta. This disturbed many Caucasians. The big farmers feared for their labor supply.

The small farmers resented the competition and a lot of wage workers were upset because the Japanese farmers tended to hire only Japanese labor. And so, in 1913, a law was enacted to prevent the Japanese from buying land. Congress banned further immigration from Japan in 1924, by which time the corporate growers had begun to recruit labor from Mexico and the Philippines.

George Shima, from his earnings as a labor contractor in the 1890's, managed to acquire land, barges, steamboats, and become a millionaire before the repressive legislation took effect. Shima employed both Japanese and Caucasians and won many friends in the Delta. He was crowned "Potato King" at a festival in Stockton.

It's 3½ miles west on the Eight Mile Road to a swing bridge on Bishop Cut. The levee road south from the bridge approaches Paradise Point, a large marina with boat rentals and a restaurant which looks out on Disappointment Slough.

We pass over the bridge and continue west across King Island two miles to a swing bridge on Honker Cut. South of this bridge, the King Island Resort has a restaurant, boat rentals, and both tent and vehicle camping. Next door is Uncle Bobbie's with the same facilities plus houseboat rentals. Both resorts and Paradise Point are convenient to some fine black bass fishing in Bishop Cut, White Slough, and Disappointment Slough. These waters are crowded with little islets and marshy berms shaped like the pieces of a picture puzzle.

The bridge on Honker Cut links King Island with the Empire Tract. The road runs two miles across the tract to the landing of the Venice Island Ferry on Connection Slough. Near the ferry landing is Herman & Helen's Resort which includes a restaurant and has fishing skiffs and houseboats for rent. A small flock of tame geese patrol the resort.

From Herman & Helen's, it's a short run by boat to good trolling and bait fishing for striped bass on the San Joaquin. There are some private duck clubs but no public facility on Venice Island where a few farm families live.

Before the Stockton Ship Channel was dredged in the years 1928-1933, the marshy reaches of the San Joaquin were dotted with the houseboats of "river rats." Some of these folk were colorful characters with names like "One-Eyed George" and "Kat-Fish Katy." But perhaps most were sober, industrious people who supported families by hunting and fishing. Such a man was Hiram P. Ward who settled on a houseboat near the Empire Tract in 1890.

Ward earned most of his income by trapping mink, otter, skunk, racoon, and beaver. Twice a year, he delivered the pelts to H. Liebes & Company in San Francisco. On these occasions, Mr. and Mrs. Ward and their daughter, Hyress, would dress up in their Sunday-go-to-meeting clothes and travel to Stockton where they'd book a stateroom on the six o'clock steamer. The voyage to San Francisco was a delight for young Hyress who recalled years later that it was like taking "a little trip to Europe." There was dancing in the social hall and it was a tremendous honor to sit at the captain's table.

14 THE STOCKTON WATERFRONT

"Today Stockton is a deep-water port, some 85 miles above the sea. But in the days of the Gold Rush steamboats, it was farther than that by a good many miles. Government dredges were yet to come, cutting straight tangents across the meanders and deepening the water so that a full-sized deepwater cargo steamer can now come to the front door of California's progressive inland seaport."

PADDLEWHEEL DAYS by Jerry McMullen, 1944

Downtown Stockton has more the look and feel of a river port than Sacramento because the old Laguna Channel of the San Joaquin penetrates the heart of the city. From the head of the channel where pleasure boats are berthed on Lake McLeod, it's only a block to City Hall and a few minutes walk to the shopping district. On the same channel, a dozen blocks west of Civic Center, is the Port of Stockton which is visited by upwards to 600 steamers a year.

What's missing at Stockton is Old Stockton—the decrepit waterfront business district remarked for its grimy skid row, colorful Chinatown, and historic brick buildings dating from the 1850's. The nine block area beloved of Hollywood directors was razed in the 1960's for redevelopment. A scattering of impressive new buildings have since risen on the site, including a flossy one-story Holiday Inn but many raw empty spaces remain.

Perhaps now the city fathers may feel a twinge of regret that at least a fragment of the old quarter was not saved for restoration as an historical park. The pity is so much that is new in Stockton is a carbon copy of what's new in scores of other California cities. This becomes evident as we approach the north side of Stockton by way of the Thornton Road and Pacific Avenue.

The Port of Stockton is visited by 400-500 freighters, tankers, and ore ships each year.

On this drive are many new sub-divisions, swank shopping centers with showy branch banks and department stores and the familiar strip cities which feature gasoline, tacos, hamburgers, and such.

From the junction of the Thornton Road with Pacific Avenue, it's less than a half mile south to Benjamin Holt Drive. West, the drive runs to the Lincoln Village Marina on Fourteen Mile Slough.

Shortly before we cross to the south bank of the Calaveras River (where the University of the Pacific shares an attractive campus with the Delta College), Pacific Avenue intersects the Brookside Road. This road approaches Buckley Cove on the Stockton Channel. At the cove is a sailing club, public launching ramp, and two large marinas which rent fishing skiffs and houseboats.

About a mile south of the river crossing, Pacific Avenue terminates on Harding Way. Here we go west ten blocks and then south on Pershing Avenue two blocks to Argonne Drive. The latter street skirts Victory Park, the site of the San Joaquin Pioneer Museum and the Haggin Art Gallery.

Argonne Drive connects with Monte Diablo Avenue which runs to Louis Park on the Stockton Channel. The park includes a public boat ramp and marina with fishing skiffs and sailboats for rent. There is a children's area known as the Pixie Woods which has baby animals, train rides, puppet shows, and a merry-go-round.

Returning to Harding Way, we proceed east to Center Street which takes us south to Civic Center and the head of the Stockton Channel. At the foot of Miner Avenue, there are two marinas with houseboat rentals. The city operates a wharf here with 48-hour berthing privileges for visitors who arrive by boat. The 196-room motel off Miner Avenue on Weber Point stands on the site of a wood and adobe house built in 1850 for Captain C. M. Weber.

In 1845, William Gulnac sold his half interest in 50,000 acres of tule flats bordering the present channel to his partner, Charles Weber, for the price of a $60 grocery bill. Gulnac had tried to colonize the land grant and failed because of the mud and mosquitoes, an epidemic of smallpox, and trouble with the Indians. Weber had better luck when he laid out a town by the channel in 1847.

The settlement was variously known as "Tuleberg" and "Mudville" until 1849 when the population zoomed to 1,000 people. It was then Weber bestowed the name Stockton for Commodore Robert F. Stockton who commanded American forces in the Mexican War. In the Gold Rush excitement, Stockton was a port for the mines and thereafter grew to prominence as the "Wheat Capitol of the World."

Probably the first paddlewheel steamer to call at Stockton was the *Merrimac* which arrived in August 1849. Regular service between Stockton and San Francisco ended when the *J. D. Peters* made her last run on Christmas Day of 1932. By then, Stockton's deep water port was nearly completed.

Now one of 31 ports in the nation equipped to handle fully containerized vessels, Stockton has berths for thirteen steamers. The most prominent dockside facility is the Stockton Elevator which is 20 stories high with a capacity for 3½ million bushels of grain. Other exports include wine, fruits, canned goods, walnuts, dairy products, honey, and copper ore from Nevada. The port is served by seven railroads.

Tours of the port are conducted from 9:00 A.M. to 3:00 P.M. It's necessary to secure reservations from Captain Coates, P. O. Box 2089, Stockton (209/466-6011). On the channel at the foot of Yosemite Street, the renowned boat builder, Stephens Marine, invites visitors during regular business hours. Most canneries in and about Stockton afford tours only for groups by special arrangement. One exception is Stokely-Van Camp at 32 East

Tokay Street in Lodi. Tours are conducted daily from 9:00 A.M. to 5:00 P.M. except on holidays.

Next door to the Port of Stockton on Rough and Ready Island is a sprawling military complex which includes a large facility of the General Services Administration. The 6,400-foot Navy wharf with seven transit sheds is the largest installation of its kind in the country. Strung along the channel is a mothball fleet of 57 ships.

Among the buildings recently completed on the site of Old Stockton is an attractive Chinese Center and a ten-story $2.8 million Filipino Community Center. Encompassing three blocks off El Dorado Street is "Little Manila" with the largest Filipino population outside the Philippines. About 40% of Stockton's population is composed of Filipino, Chinese, Japanese, Hindu, Black, Mexican, Basque, Portuguese, and Italian Americans.

Despite all the new construction, much of Stockton's downtown area appears shabby and passe. Many merchants have been hard hit by competition from the new suburban shopping centers. Business suffers and welfare rolls mushroom during the winter slack season when thousands of farm and food industry workers living in the city cannot find employment.

Of the many motion pictures filmed in the Stockton area, the first to show Stockton as Stockton was John Huston's "Fat City," which was but faintly applauded by the Chamber of Commerce. Despite the demolition of the old quarter, Stockton continues to average $1 million a year by hosting Hollywood location companies. In 1972, the Delta's movie capitol provided locations for Stanley Kramer's "Oklahoma Crude."

Stockton has long suffered the reputation as "a dull Valley workshop," yet it has opera, a full season of live theatre, and a symphony orchestra conducted by Kyung Soo Won who also leads the Philharmonic Orchestra in Seoul. Rock groups proliferate and New Orleans music is kept alive by the Delta and

Pacific Jazz Bands. As for North Beach topless and triple X movies, Stockton has some of that as well as good nightclubs and restaurants. The city operates two golf courses, seven swimming pools, 24 parks, 78 tennis courts, and an Olympic size indoor ice skating rink.

Stockton provides the base for a county-wide program of low cost private patient care which includes mobile clinics to serve migrant farm workers. A new county library is stocked with 350,000 books and 1,000 periodicals. Among the city's 110 places of worship is a lovely Buddhist temple set in an Oriental garden near Smith Canal. The rapidly expanding University of the Pacific is the oldest chartered institution of higher learning in California. Delta College was among the first in the nation to offer courses in ecology.

15 ROBERTS ISLAND

"You find an in-between kind of Delta island where people live in cottages or shacks far from everything and everybody, keeping a few goats or hogs and doing Lord knows what for a living. Some of this kind of halfway ground between mechanized farm and tangled wilderness has been taken over by yacht clubs and duck clubs. Some of it surrounds the ferry landings and the little fishing-boat harbors. But it's all Huckleberry Finn Country, where the postman never rings twice or even once—but toots the horn of his boat to announce the mail has arrived."

SUNSET by the Travel Department, 1959

South from Stockton's Civic Center by way of Center Street, it's less than a mile to Charter Way. Here we turn west to follow State Route 4 about 2½ miles to the Garwood Bridge on the main channel of the San Joaquin. Across the river is the largest island in the Delta.

Roberts Island approximates 100 square miles. In the 1870's, the principal landowner was General T. H. Williams who also owned much of 45,000-acre Union Island and part of Grand Island, as well as 20,000 acres abound Clarksburg. Williams was denounced as a "land hog" by some in the Delta who resented his employment of Chinese labor.

Lonely is the word for Roberts Island notwithstanding part of it lies within the city limits of Stockton. On the six mile drive to Holt, the vistas are mostly of flat open fields, grazed in places by sheep or cattle. Nowhere on the islands of the southern Delta are there settlements larger than hamlet-size. Here and there, you see a weathered barn, an old packing shed, and the modest dwellings of farm workers and ranch foremen. Now, as in the

*Asparagus on Roberts Island. Harvesting begins
in March and is normally completed by the
Fourth of July. This field has gone to seed.*

first days of reclamation, much of the acreage is owned by large corporations.

It's easy to miss Holt if you happen to glance on the wrong side of the road when you get there. There is a lone bar and grill signed "The Delta Cafe." Holt is a station on the Atchison, Topeka and Santa Fe Railroad, named for Charles Parker Holt who operated a farm on Roberts Island. In a garage on the farm, Holt's brother, Benjamin, invented a tractor that wouldn't sink in the Delta's light peat soil. When the machine was demonstrated in 1905, someone remarked how it resembled "a great caterpillar." The tanks used by the British in World War II were developed from "Uncle Ben" Holt's caterpillar tractor.

Behind the Delta Cafe, we find the junction of the Holt and Lower Jones Roads. It's five miles north on the Holt Road to a junction with the Neugerbauer Road on the levee which fronts the Stockton Ship Channel. The levee road east approaches the Windmill Cove Marina on Vulcan Island. This resort includes vehicle camping, houseboat rentals, and a seafood restaurant with windows looking out on the ship channel. There's still a windmill at Windmill Cove, one of hundreds used to drain the islands before they were made obsolete by electric pumps.

West, the Neugerbauer Road passes fields of tomatoes, corn, and asparagus. Tomatoes are the No. 1 canning crop in the Delta, which produces nearly all the tomato paste and half the catsup consumed in the United States.

In 1963, the Delta tomato harvest was accomplished by 42,400 workers, most of whom were Mexican nationals. In 1969, several years after the bracero program was terminated, 97% of the crop was machine harvested. Where there used to be 3-4 pickings by hand, the tomato harvester removes the plants as well as the tomatoes. A crew of women on the machine sort the fruit on a conveyor belt which delivers the mature tomatoes to trucks moving alongside the harvester. There's considerable waste.

Growers hope, however, to cut their losses through use of a plant hormone which, when sprayed on the plants, promotes uniform ripening of the crop.

A special hybrid tomato, tough enough to endure machine handling had to be perfected before mechanical harvesters could be used. The machines are so costly they cannot be made to pay on farms of less than 100 acres. The Delta harvest peaks from mid-September through mid-October. Most tomatoes on the islands are grown on leased land and are purchased by the canneries before they are grown. This is known as "forward buying," whereas crops grown on speculation are spoken of as "open acreage."

A mile or so west on the Neugerbauer Road, the levee bends to Turner Cut, where we see "the longest houseboat in the Delta." It's an old San Francisco fire barge purchased by Eric and Olga Ehrichs in 1950 after they retired from operating a chain of soda fountains. A bit farther, we arrive at Ehrich's Resort which has a restaurant, boat rentals, and vehicle camping. It's another mile to the Turner Cut Resort. This landing has a store, restaurant, boat rentals, vehicle camping, and overnight accommodations.

A little farther near the slip for the MacDonald Island Ferry is the Tiki Lagun Marina, a large resort with a South Sea Islands decor. There's a store, houseboat rentals, tent and vehicle camping, snack bar and restaurant.

To approach the Lost Isle Marina, we ride the ferry to MacDonald Island and proceed north up the levee two miles to Acker Island, located on the Stockton Channel at the mouth of Turner Cut. A ferry operates to Acker Island where tame goats graze the grounds of the Lost Isle Club. The resort includes tent camping, boat rentals, a bar and restaurant, and a sandy swimming beach.

Not much has been said about swimming in this guide

because it's not overly popular in the Delta. There's nothing against swimming except the water appears slightly murky even in summer.

Off the tip of MacDonald Island, the Delta Yacht Club occupies Tule Island and the St. Francis Yacht Club has a place on Tinsley Island. Near Acker Island, the Weber Point Yacht Club is based on Spud Island which is an undeveloped county park. The Army Engineers have designated Spud Island a "spoils area," which means silt will be dumped on it when and if the Engineers carry out their plan to deepen the Stockton Channel by five feet. The project was delayed pending an environmental study. When the original channel was dug, the habitat of mink, otter, and other fur-bearing animals was destroyed.

On MacDonald Island is the 3,000-acre Whiskey Slough Farms, Incorporated, which is owned by the Zuckerman family. About 700 acres on the ranch compose one of the largest "organic farms" in the west. Here an entomologist is employed to use natural insect predators in place of chemical pesticides. Norwegian seaweed, chicken manure, and ground rock phosphate are substituted for chemical fertilizers. The farm grows asparagus, corn, potatoes, tomatoes, broccoli, carrots, zucchini, bell peppers, melons, and 39 other crops.

From the Tiki Lagun Marina Resort on Roberts Island, the MacDonald Road follows the levee south one mile and then bears east four miles to a junction with the Holt Road.

Middle River boat livery.

16 THE JONES TRACT

"There are at least 500 World War II surplus Army GMC trucks still in use on the islands. Jesus (Cahuacha) Alvarado, 46, head mechanic for a fleet of 20 of the old trucks on Mandeville Island says he came to Mandeville Island with the antique vehicles. 'Island owners brought the trucks here in 1945 when the war ended. I've kept them running ever since. The trucks never leave the island. Since they don't go on public roads, they don't need license plates.'"

LOS ANGELES TIMES by Charles Hillinger, 1970

From the junction of the Holt and Lower Jones Road near State Highway 4, it's a short drive west on the Lower Jones Road to Whiskey Slough Harbor. This landing has a restaurant, boat rentals (including canoes and kayaks), vehicle camping and overnight accommodations. The resort rents some stationary houseboats which were formerly the homes of "river rats." Whiskey Slough is a slender, protected waterway, covered in places with water hyacinths.

The Lower Jones Road runs up Whiskey Slough on the levee of the Jones Tract 3½ miles north to the Empire Cut. Among the crops we are likely to see on this drive are asparagus, a member of the lily family which was a delicacy in ancient Rome. Not long ago, the Delta supplied 90% of the world's canned asparagus. Now there's competition from Taiwan and Mexico, as well as Monterey, Imperial, and Riverside Counties. However, San Joaquin County remains the state's leading producer with a crop valued in 1970 at $16 million. Formerly, much of the crop was white asparagus, which is still popular in West Germany.

Asparagus is an expensive crop because the stoop labor it requires accounts for 45% of the gross income. Harvesting the spears with a forked knife is difficult work demanding a fair amount of skill. This was a specialty of the Filipinos who arrived in the Delta mostly through the years 1923 to 1929. As the Filipinos began to climb the economic ladder, the asparagus growers filled the gap with Mexican nationals. After the bracero program was terminated in 1964, mechanical harvesting was tried with mediocre results. The machines now available are too expensive for use on tracts of less than 50 acres.

The Delta asparagus harvest takes place from March through June, at which time the labor force peaks at 15,000.

The Empire Cut divides the north end of the Jones Tract from Mildred and MacDonald Islands. Along the Empire Cut, fishermen may be seen relaxing on the levee in canvas folding chairs. Mostly catfish and black bass are caught in the southern Delta. Just after we pass the landing of the Mildred Island Ferry (which is private), we come to Middle River. This is the longest primitive waterway in the Delta. It contains many islets and marshy berms.

Shortly, we arrive at the swing bridge which crosses Middle River to Bacon Island. Blackberries grow so thickly along the levees of Bacon Island, they may be picked from a boat. The Sam Huey family on Bacon Island are among the last Chinese to farm the Delta. They grow potatoes on a thousand acres. A private drawbridge links Bacon Island with Mandeville Island which is owned and farmed by Alfred Zuckerman.

For the sum of $500, hunters may enjoy two days of shooting on Mandeville Island in the duck season. Zuckerman has two ponds planted with corn to attract the birds. There are scores of private clubs but no public shooting grounds in the southern Delta. On the Jones Tract, a group of Stockton business and professional men own a 750-acre farm which yields asparagus but mainly represents an investment in good hunting. One hundred acres of corn are planted just for the birds.

With so much feed and water on the islands, the unattached hunter who tries to freelance on the lakes and sloughs needs a lot of luck. On Sherman Lake, hunters lay out as many as 1,000 decoys and even then the shooting, at best, is only fair.

Mandeville Island, which covers 5,440 acres, was probably named for James W. Mandeville who was a state senator and U. S. Surveyor General. When the levee on Mandeville Island broke in the high water of 1938, the old paddlewheel steamers, *Onisbo, Reform,* and *Navajo*, were towed in to plug the dike. Then the *J. D. Peters,* which still had power, was positioned so its paddlewheel could be used to push water off the island. After Mandeville was drained, the stranded steamers were used as barracks for farm workers.

Off the north end of Mandeville Island is an islet known as Mandeville Tip. This is an undeveloped county park which has picnic tables and restrooms but no water. It's another "spoils area" which the county hopes to develop for recreation after the Army Engineers finish dredging the ship channel.

From the Bacon Island Bridge, it's a country mile down the levee to the sleepy hamlet of Middle River (population 25). There's an old wharf and warehouse on the Santa Fe Railroad here and some small landings. Dinty Moore's and Pop's Boats have bait, motors, and fishing skiffs for rent. The weathered Middle River Inn has an air-conditioned snack bar.

Two miles farther south, we come to the landing of the Woodward Island Ferry. This ferry and the MacDonald, Venice, and Staten Island Ferries are operated by San Joaquin County, whereas the two ferries which serve Ryer Island are state operated. Before an epidemic of bridge building occurred in the 1930's and 1940's, the Delta was served by scores of public ferries.

Posted near the Woodward Island ferry slip and elsewhere on the levees are signs warning the traveler to be careful with matches. Numerous peat fires were started in paddlewheel days by sparks blown ashore from passing steamers. Peat fires tend to go underground and, when this happens, they are impossible to put out except by flooding. However, the farmers often used to burn their fields to remove stubble or kill blight. Each time, several inches of the precious peat soil were consumed.

Now, with the annual loss of soil to the winds and the slow subsidence of the islands caused by the weight of the levees, the farmers have a lot to worry about. Already there are places on the islands where the water table is so close to the surface, few if any crops may be grown. However, a study team funded by the Ford Foundation recently came up with a brilliant solution. San Francisco has a garbage disposal problem. So why not barge the garbage to the islands and mix it with the soil as compost? Both San Francisco and the farmers seem to feel the idea is worth looking into.

Just south of the Woodward Island Ferry is Vern's Place with boats and motors for rent. We turn east at the ferry slip on the Bacon Island Road and proceed five miles to a swing bridge which crosses Trapper Slough to State Highway 4. Near the bridge is Uncle Tom's Cabin, a boat landing with a restaurant.

17 TRACY

"Why should the Bay-Delta area be sacrificed to accommodate a doubled Southern California population desired by nobody but real estate promoters. The answer, of course, is in the obsolete myth that the goal of every community must be galloping growth. To grow we must 'conquer' nature, which means filling bays, leveling the hills, paving the deserts."
SUNDAY EXAMINER & CHRONICLE by Harold Gilliam, 1969

The Tracy Road leaves California Highway 4 three miles southwest of Holt. About two miles south of the junction, the road crosses a swing bridge on Middle River to Union Island which is the second largest island in the Delta.

From Middle River, the road slices across cultivated fields five miles to a swing bridge on the Fabian and Grant Line Canals. Union Island ranks high in the production of tomatoes but here as elsewhere in the Delta the crops are diversified.

A crop easily confused with yellow corn when it first sprouts in the fields is milo, a variety of sorghum used for stock feed. Here and there, the farms are given a splash of color by a field of yellow safflower or sunflower. Both crops are grown for their seed from which oil is extracted.

The operators of the machines observed at harvest time include black people who first arrived on the Coast in World War II to work in the shipyards. The pattern of farm employment in the Delta has changed in recent years. The big ranches have tended to provide more year around jobs for welders, mechanics, machinists, and skilled equipment operators, as well as agronomists, entomologists, accountants, and ranch supervisors.

At the same time, opportunities for unskilled work have dwindled. Many migrant workers are finding it impossible to support a family on their earnings from the fields. In 1969, it was estimated 59% of 486,700 farm workers in California earn less than $1,000 a year. In 1971, the State Division of Rural Manpower Services reported an increase in the number of migrant workers and more people seeking work than there were job openings.

For seasonal labor, there's been a growing reliance on housewives and young people. Mechanization with such new devices as pneumatic pruning shears has made farm work more attractive to women. The old style barracks and labor camps—shabby places noted for their bad sanitation and often filled with black widow spiders—are becoming obsolete in the Delta. It's more usual for labor contractors to bus crews from Stockton or Sacramento.

Off the Tracy Road west on the levee of the Grant Line Canal is the Tracy Oasis which includes a restaurant, vehicle camping, launching, and boat rentals. The marina is convenient to the Salmon Slough area recently proposed as a state park. Across the drawbridge on the Fabian Tract, the Grimes Road runs west to Tony's Boat Harbor on the Fabian & Bell Canal. Tony's has launching, boat rentals, and vehicle camping.

Shortly, we cross Old River to the mainland of the old Rancho Pescadero. The name originated with a Spanish expedition of 1810-11 who observed Yokut Indians fishing the stream. About two-thirds of the flow of the San Joaquin enters the Delta through Old River.

Off the Tracy Road approximately three miles from Old River, the Holly Road bears east to Sugar Cut. Here the refinery wharf of the Holly Sugar Company is served by barges which come down Old River.

A little farther we pass beneath the new Interstate 205 which allows traffic on US 50 to bypass Tracy. Old US 50 runs through the heart of the business district. Tracy (population 15,000) was

Farm near Byron.

founded in 1878 as a station on the Southern Pacific line to Berkeley. There are good motels and restaurants but little else to hold the traveler at Tracy. Owens Illinois, H. J. Heinz, and Laura Scudders' are among the companies which have large plants in the area. The Tracy Defense Depot employs 2,100 people.

On the east side of Tracy, the new Interstate 5 freeway spans the San Joaquin River at the site of an historic ford known as "El Paso del Pescadero." Before the Gold Rush, the main trail leading down the Sierra to the Bay Area crossed here. In high water months previous to 1844, mountain men hired the Indians to ferry them across on tule rafts. Gabriel Moraga came this way in 1810 on a search for mission sites. It was Moraga who named the San Joaquin for Saint Joachim and the Sacramento for the Holy Sacrament.

Now known as Mossdale, the old ford marks the limit of tidal action on the San Joaquin. The mean difference in the tide at Stockton is 3.2 feet and at Sacramento 2.4 feet. Upriver from Mossdale, the San Joaquin is navigable during the high water months to Hills Ferry on the Merced-Stanislaus County Line. There are a dozen drawbridges which require up to a week's notice to be opened. In low water months, the head of navigation is the railway bridge near Lathrop.

Although Stockton was declared the head of navigation in the 1860's, there was traffic on the San Joaquin for many years. Sternwheelers called at landings on the Tuolumne and Stanislaus Rivers as late as the 1870's. Service to Firebaugh on Fresno Slough was maintained until 1906.

A mile or so above Mossdale, the Islander Marina and Wetherbee Lake Resort are based on Walthall Slough. To get here, you cross the Interstate 5 bridge and exit to Highway 120 where you turn right on McKinley Avenue at the first stop light.

On the final leg of this Delta tour, we leave Tracy on the Byron Highway which is County Route J-4. It's six miles to Bethany which used to have a wharf on Old River. It was a shipping point for coal mined south of Tracy at Corral Hollow.

About three miles farther, on the extreme northeast corner of Alameda County, we turn north on the Lindeman Road. Shortly we arrive at Del's Boat Harbor on Old River. The resort has launching, boat rentals, and a restaurant. Along the levee near Del's are many summer cottages and a new kind of stationary houseboat — luxury mobile homes mounted on pontoons. A stone's throw from Del's is the Delta-Mendota Canal by which the Central Valley Project delivers water to the upper San Joaquin Valley.

At the entrance to the canal is a huge fish screen which cost $2 million to build. Thousands of baby salmon and striped bass drawn here by the CVP pumps are collected in tanker trucks and restored to the river at places remote from the canal. An argument for the proposed Peripheral Canal is that it would eliminate pumping from the Delta.

Returning to the Byron Highway, it's a mile to Contra Costa County. Three miles farther, the Clifton Road forks west to the Lazy Marina on Italian Slough. A bit further is Clifton Court, a tract which was flooded to provide a forebay for the California Aqueduct. No boats are allowed on the lake except during the hunting season. An aerial count of ducks and geese in November 1972 reported 870,000 birds in the Delta, of which a majority were found on Clifton Court, Bethany Reservoir, and flooded Andrus Island. The pumping plant for the California Aqueduct is located near Bethany Reservoir a short distance west of the Byron Highway.

At the heart of the Peripheral Canal controversy is the question whether or not the rich land of the Delta should be sacrificed so land in the upper San Joaquin Valley may be irrigated and Los Angeles may continue to grow.

Before the Gold Rush, the Delta received from the rivers a

flow of 30 million acre feet each year. This was the run-off from 46,500 square miles of California. Such was the "hydraulic barrier" created by the river flow that salt water was confined to lower San Francisco Bay. But now, because of upstream diversions for industry and agriculture, the flow has been reduced to less than 18 million acre feet a year and the salt water has moved up to Antioch. When and if the State Water Project is completed, it's anticipated the flow might be reduced to as little as 3 million acre feet in a dry year.

The Peripheral Canal would obtain water from the Sacramento at Hood and transport it directly to the Delta-Mendota Canal and California Aqueduct. Critics say this diversion of good water and the increased amounts of waste water entering the Delta by way of the San Joaquin would have the effect of turning the Delta into a giant cesspool.

Perhaps the Achilles heel of the multi-billion dollar State Water Project is the lack of provision for drainage. Farmers must flush their fields to avoid a build-up of salt in the soil. It's believed an imbalance of salt caused the demise of ancient civilizations in the Tigris and Euphrates Valleys. The problem is what to do with the waste water that is loaded with salt, nutrients, and pesticides. There was a plan to build a 290-mile canal which would dump the waste water in the lower Delta. This drew a storm of protest from Contra Costa County and the plan was scrapped.

Presently, the San Joaquin is used as a drain which may be the reason striped bass fishing is mediocre in the southern Delta. The waste water is diluted by infusion of fresh water from the Friant and Delta-Mendota Canals. But, even so, farmers who draw irrigation from the San Joaquin have been heard to complain the water is of low quality. Unhappily, the more good water the state delivers to farmers on the dry west side of the San Joaquin Valley, the more inferior water must be returned to the Delta.

A problem that is on the way to solution is the 20 million gallons of raw sewage discharged by freighters and pleasure boats into the Delta each year. In 1972, the Environmental Protection Agency set standards which will eventually require all boats to have self-contained sanitary systems. The "no discharge" policy will take years to fully implement, partly because existing vessels will be allowed the option to install treatment devices.

There is localized pollution in the Delta such as is found at the outfalls of canneries and there is occasional pollution such as occurs at Carquinez Strait during an extreme minus tide. But Fish and Game biologists engaged in a wildlife study of the Delta recently reported there was no "general" pollution and that the water quality was better than in most estuaries surrounded by cities.

December fishing on Frank's Tract.

18 BETHEL ISLAND

"One of the chief reasons for the popularity of striped bass angling is that somewhere in the great delta area not a day goes by, year around, that someone doesn't tangle with old linesides. During the fall and winter months when trout are generally illegal and warm-water fishing is slow, striper invasions reach the peak in many areas."

OUTDOOR LIFE by William Curtis, 1957

Byron used to be the busiest shipping point for produce in eastern Contra Costa County. Now it's a tired little trading place with cracked sidewalks. Two miles south of town (about a mile from the Lindeman Road), a road leaves the west side of the highway for Byron Hot Springs. Indians enjoyed the waters here before a fashionable spa was established in 1868. The hotel burned in 1912 but was rebuilt and still stands on grounds occasionally used for fairs and festivals.

Two miles above Byron is the junction with State Highway 4. A short way east off Route 4 is Discovery Bay, a luxury "second home" development built around lagoons adjoining Indian Slough. A bit farther at Old River is Alex Boat Harbor which has fishing skiffs for rent. From Old River, the highway crosses Victoria Island to the Union Point Resort on Middle River. The resort includes a restaurant and boat rentals.

Continuing north on the Byron Highway through lush orchard country, it's a half-mile to the Marsh Creek Road. Some distance up this road is the stone house built in 1856 for Dr. John Marsh, who purchased the Rancho Los Medanos in 1837.

A mile farther, Route 4 leaves the Byron Highway for Brentwood which was named for John Marsh's ancestral home in

Essex, England. Brentwood thrives as a shipping center for almonds and other produce.

Opposite the road to Brentwood on the east side of the Byron Highway, the Point-of-Timber Road approaches the site of an old schooner landing on Indian Slough.

Three miles farther north, the Orwood Road leaves for the Orwood Resort on Indian Slough. This is a large establishment with a motel, restaurant, tent and vehicle camping, and houseboat rentals. Indian Slough is good water for catfish, crappie, black bass, and "sunnies."

Two miles above Orwood, the Byron Highway terminates on the Delta Road. East of the junction is Rock Slough where cities on Suisun Bay obtain their water supply by way of the Contra Costa Canal. When Andrus Island flooded in 1972, the "hydraulic barrier" off Antioch was disrupted and salt water spread far into the Delta. For a month or so, the water in the Contra Costa Canal was too salty to drink.

We motor west on the Delta Road two miles to Knightsen and then two miles north on the Knightsen Road to Cypress Road. East on Cypress, it's 3½ miles to the Bethel Island Road.

Bethel Island contains the largest resort development in the Delta. There are too many places to name, but the list includes trailer parks, campgrounds, motels, summer cottages, floating restaurants, bars, yacht clubs, boat liveries, bait shops, houseboat rentals and sales, as well as yacht brokers, marine supply houses, engine overhaul shops, and even a landing that specializes in propeller repair.

Shortly before we arrive on Bethel Island, a road leads east to several landings on Sandmound Slough. Resorts crowd the levee east and west of the bridge on Dutch Slough. Across the bridge is the village of Bethel Island. Here Stone and Taylor Slough Roads approach more resorts. Just north of town, the Gateway Road bears east alongside a public golf course to

Mike Hayden fishing for panfish
on Snodgrass Slough.

restaurants and marinas on the levee which fronts Frank's Tract.

Despite all the development, much of Bethel Island's 3,554 acres is given over to cattle grazing.

Frank's Tract was a farmed island, about the same size as Bethel Island, before the levee broke in the winter of 1937-38. Now the tract is a state park which lies mostly underwater. Only the extreme western tip of Frank's Tract remains dry. It's undeveloped and accessible only by boat.

Frank's Tract is a fisherman's park remarked as one of the better places to try for striped bass in mid-winter.

Stripers are by far the most sought after game fish in the lower Delta. Those caught in winter and early spring average ten pounds in weight. The record for the Delta is a 65-pounder hooked on the San Joaquin in 1951. These fish are gourmet fare when baked or broiled in a wine sauce. But mostly it's the remarkable sporting quality of stripers which endears them to fishermen. When hooked, even a modest five-pounder may be counted on to afford the angler terrific sport with fierce lunges and powerful runs.

The striper is a voracious feeder but also a wary, temperamental fish, especially in winter when near freezing water temperatures dull his appetite. At such times, a sliding sinker rig is needed because, if the striper detects the slightest resistance when he takes the bait, he'll drop it and leave.

Since flooded islands, such as Frank's Tract, have no current, they may be fished without a sinker when the water is calm. Some of the old timers at Frank's Tract use a method known as "half dollar fishing." After the bait is cast, perhaps 20 feet of line is stripped from the reel and coiled on one of the seats in the boat. A fifty cent piece is placed over the coil to hold it in place. When a fish takes the bait and the line begins to peel off the coil, the fisherman does nothing. The striper may be only playing with the bait. Usually, it's best to wait until all the line in the coil is gone before attempting to set the hook.

The popular baits include Pacific sardine, "glass shrimp," and sandworms imported from Maine. The hook size may vary from 1/0 to 6/0, depending on the type of bait used. Light salt water spinning tackle is popular, but many striper enthusiasts still prefer the traditional boat rod, 6½ to 7½ feet, and star drag reel spooled with 20-30 pound test monofilament line.

In late spring, adult stripers move down to the lower bay and coastal waters. A high percentage of stripers hooked in the Delta during summer fall short of the legal 16-inch minimum length. The daily creel limit is three fish. For years, the state has been tagging stripers as part of a study to determine how the fishery should be managed. Anglers are requested to mail any tags they find to the Fish and Game Department. Some tags bring a reward of $5. Of 19,000 stripers tagged in 1972, about 900 had $5 tags.

A study in the 1960's by the Stanford Research Institute found that the striper fishery yields the state $7 million a year in recreational values. These include what a fisherman spends on gas, boat rentals, lodging, and so forth. Stripers are prolific. A twelve-pounder may spawn a million eggs in a season. The newly hatched eggs drift in the current for a couple days and, unhappily, many are lost to diversions, such as the California Aqueduct. In recent years, the striper population in the Bay and Delta has fluctuated between a million and 1½ million adult fish.

Most striper fishing is done from boats. However, the Delta is not a place for the novice to go out alone on the main waterways in a small boat. The beginner is better advised to rent or launch a boat on a protected slough and not venture far from shore. The lakes and ship channels may appear as smooth as glass at dawn only to be torn by whitecaps an hour later. It takes time to know the hazards, which include snags, riptides, tule fogs, and blind corners where fishermen should never anchor for risk of being overrun by a powerboat coming from the opposite direction. Many resorts located on big water, such as Frank's Tract, refuse to rent boats to persons without navigation experience.

Sheriff's patrol boats cruise the main channels to enforce boating laws and assist parties with motor breakdowns. Usually, the trouble is an empty gas tank.

Leaving Bethel Island, we return to the Cypress Road and bear west to Oakley, a shipping center for grapes on the Santa Fe line. A road to take out of Oakley in February is O'Hara Avenue. It's three miles to Lone Tree Way which affords an aerial view of the almond orchards in flower.

Two miles west of Oakley on Highway 4, a road leaves north for the Big Break Resort which has a restaurant, launching, and boat rentals. The Big Break is an island flooded years ago and never reclaimed.

Our tour of the Delta Country is nearly ended. Antioch lies just up the road.

BIBLIOGRAPHY

Adams, Leon. *Striped Bass Fishing.* Palo Alto: Pacific Books, 1954.

Boyle, Graves, and Watkins. *The Water Hustlers.* San Francisco: The Sierra Club, 1971.

Cook, Fred S. *Steamboats in the Valley.* Volcano, California: California Traveler, 1971.

Chu, George. *"Chinatowns in the Delta."* The California Historical Society Quarterly, March 1970.

Dana, Julian, *The Sacramento — River of Gold.* New York: Farrar and Rinehart, 1939.

Forbes, Jack D. *Native Americans of California and Nevada.* Healdsburg, California: Naturegraph Publishers, 1969.

Galarza, Ernesto. *Merchants of Labor.* Charlotte/Santa Barbara: McNally and Loftus, 1964.

Gardner, Erle Stanley. *Gypsy Days on the Delta.* New York: William Morrow and Co., Inc., 1967.

Gardner, Erle Stanley. *Drifting Down the Delta.* New York: William Morrow and Co., Inc., 1969.

Gardner, Erle Stanley. *World of Water.* New York: William Morrow and Co., Inc., 1965.

Gilliam, Harold. *San Francisco Bay.* Garden City, New York: Doubleday and Company, Inc., 1957.

Girdner and Loftis. *The Great Betrayal.* Toronto: The MacMillan Company, 1969.

Gudde, Erwin G. *California Place Names.* Berkeley: University of California Press, 1965.

Hoover, Rensch, and Abeloe. *Historic Spots in California.* Stanford, California: Stanford University Press, 1966.

Kelley, D. W. *"Ecological Studies of the Sacramento-San Joaquin Estuary,"* Part I, Fish Bulletin 133. Sacramento: California Department of Fish and Game, 1966.

Kroeger, A. L. *Handbook of the Indians of California.* Berkeley: California Book Company, Ltd., 1953.

Lantis, Steiner, and Karinen. *California.* Belmont, California: Wadsworth Publishing Co., 1963.

Lord, Myrtle Shaw. *A Sacramento Saga.* Sacramento: Sacramento Chamber of Commerce, 1946.

MacFisher, Purcell. *History of Contra Costa County.* Berkeley: Gillick Press, 1940.

MacMullen, Jerry. *Paddlewheel Days in California.* Stanford: Stanford University Press, 1946.

McGowan, Joseph A. *History of the Sacramento Valley.* New York and West Palm Beach: Lewis Historical Publishing Company, 1961.

McWilliams, Carey. *Factories in the Field.* Boston: Little, Brown and Company, 1939.

Miller, Ron and Peggy. *Delta Country.* Glendale: La Siesta Press, 1971.

Minick, Roger. *Delta West.* Berkeley: Scrimshaw Press, 1969.

Skinner, John E. *"An Historical Review of the Fish and Wildlife Resources of the San Francisco Bay Area,"* Water Projects Branch Report No. 1. Sacramento: California Department of Fish and Game, 1962.

Stevens, Larry. *Chinese Americans.* Stockton (P. O. Box 794, 95201): Hammer Press, 1970.

Turner, Jerry L. and Kelley, D. W. *"Ecological Studies of the Sacramento-San Joaquin Delta, Part II, Fishes of the Delta,"* Fish Bulletin 136, Sacramento: California Department of Fish and Game, 1966.

Tyson, James L. *Diary of a Physician in California.* Oakland: Biobooks, 1955.

––. *California Agriculture.* Claude B. Hutchison, Editor. Berkeley: University of California Press, 1946.

––. *California Water,* David Seckler, Editor. Berkeley: University of California Press, 1971.

––. *History of Sacramento County, California.* Oakland: Thompson and West, 1880. Reprinted Berkeley: Howell-North, 1960.

––. *History of San Joaquin County, California.* Oakland: Thompson and West, 1879. Reprinted Berkeley: Howell-North, 1968.

––. *History of Yolo County, California.* Woodland, California: William O. Russell, Editor, 1940.

––. *Illustrations of Contra Costa County, California.* Oakland: Smith and Elliott, 1879 (?). Reprinted: Contra Costa County Historical Society, 1952.

––. *Let's Go, A Family Guide to Fun in the Bay Area.* Richmond, California: American Association of University Women, Richmond Chamber of Commerce.

BOATING
ABC's of California Boating Law, Resources Agency, Sacramento 95814.

Bay and Delta Yachtsman (published monthly), P. O. Box 819, Rio Vista, California 94571

Boating & Fishing Almanac, Northern California and Nevada, Box 344, Venice, California 90291

The Sacramento Lock — Your Key to Safe Lockage, Corps of Engineers, 650 Capitol Mall, Sacramento, California 95814

Safe Boating on the Sacramento River, California Resources Agency, Department of Navigation and Ocean Development, Sacramento, California 95814.

Sunset: Where to Go Boating in California. Lane Magazine and Book Company, Menlo Park, 1972 (annual).

WEATHER

National Weather Service station at Jackson Butte (162.4 MHz) weather information for the Delta area.

MAPS

The California Delta (Map), Weekend Outdoor Productions, P. O. Box 878, Oakland, California 94604

Chart of Sacramento-San Joaquin Rivers; Pittsburg to Antioch and Horseshoe Bend, Kym's Guide, Triumph Press, 1972.

Chart of San Joaquin River; Frank's Tract to Stockton, Kym's Guide, Triumph Press, 1968.

Contra Costa, Yolo, Solano, Sacramento, and San Joaquin Counties (Maps), Harry Freese, Oakland, California.

Delta Region, Delta Marina Yacht Harbor, Rio Vista, California.

Golden Gate Atlas: 1971, Marine Exchange of San Francisco Bay Region.

Outdoor Trails Guide Book, Wildlife & Recreation Services, P. O. Box 21-4152, Sacramento, California, 1966.

Sacramento River and the Delta Area (Maps), Johnson Maps, Fremont, California.

Striped Bass Fishing Map, Department of Fish and Game, 1969.

NAUTICAL CHARTS

Published annually by the U. S. Department of Commerce:

Nautical Chart 165-SC: San Francisco Bay to Antioch.

Nautical Chart 666: Sacramento River. Sacramento to Colusa.

Nautical Chart 5528-SC: Sacramento River. Andrus Island to Sacramento.

Nautical Chart 5527-SC: Lower Sacramento River and San Joaquin River.

NEWSPAPERS

River News Herald and Isleton Journal
San Francisco Examiner
San Francisco Chronicle
Sacramento Bee
Sacramento Union

Oakland Tribune
Stockton Record
Tracy Press
Antioch Ledger
Los Angeles Times
Lodi-News Sentinel

REPORTS AND BULLETINS

California Agriculture, published monthly by University of California Division of Agricultural Services, Berkeley, California.

The California State Water Project Summary: 1969, Bulletin No. 132-70, Department of Water Resources, Sacramento, California 1970.

Commercial Fish Catch of California for the Year 1947, Fish Bulletin No. 74, Bureau of Marine Fisheries, 1949.

Fish and Wildlife Appendix C— Report to the Water Authority of the State of California on Feasibility of Construction by the State of Barriers in the San Francisco Bay System, California Department of Public Works, Division of Water Resources, June 1955.

Inter-Agency Ecological Study Program for the Sacramento-San Joaquin Estuary. Cooperative study by California Fish and Game Department, Department of Water Resources, U. S. Bureau of Sport Fisheries and Wildlife, and U. S. Bureau of Reclamation. First annual report, 1971.

Preview of the California Water Plan, State Water Resources Board, March 1956.

Rural Manpower Report 1971, California Department of Human Resources.

INFORMATION SOURCES

Antioch Chamber of Commerce, 707 "A" Street, Antioch 94509 (415/757-1800).

California Department of Parks and Recreation, P. O. Box 2390, Sacramento 95811 (916/445-6477).

California State Chamber of Commerce, 455 Capitol Mall, Sacramento 95814.

Tracy District Chamber of Commerce, P.O. Box 891, Tracy, California 95376. (209/835-2131)

Sacramento Chamber of Commerce, 917 Seventh Street, P.O. Box 1017, Sacramento, California 95805

Greater Stockton Chamber of Commerce, 1105 North El Dorado Street, Stockton 95202. (209/466-7076)

U.S. Coast Guard Station—Delta, 900 South Second Street, Rio Vista 94571 (707/374-2655).

Isleton Chamber of Commerce, P.O. Box 397, Isleton, California 95641 (916/777-6221).

Thornton Chamber of Commerce, P. O. Box 146, Thornton 95686.

Region II, California Fish and Game Department, 1001 Jedsmith Drive, Sacramento.

Department of Water Resources, 1416 Ninth Street, Sacramento 95814.

Department of Agriculture, 1220 N Street, Sacramento 95814.

U. S. Bureau of Reclamation, Region 2, Sacramento 95812.

Department of Navigation and Ocean Development, 1416 Ninth Street, Sacramento 95814.

Bethel Island Chamber of Commerce, Bethel Island, California 94511 (415/684-2586).

Rio Vista Chamber of Commerce, 11 North Front Street, Rio Vista, California 94571 (707/374-2700).

Pittsburgh Chamber of Commerce, 1901 Railroad Avenue, Pittsburg, California 94565 (415/432-7301).

Friends of Clarksburg Youth Pheasant Hunting Co-op, c/o Mike Campbell, Route 1, P.O. Box 321, Clarksburg, California 95612 (916/775-1227).

Corps of Engineers, 650 Capitol Mall, Sacramento, California 95814 (916/449-2341).

INDEX

124